G000123334

A Disciple's Journal
Year B

Advent 2020, 2023, 2026, 2029

A Guide for Daily Prayer,
Bible Reading, and Discipleship

Steven W. Manskar
with Melanie C. Gordon
& Taylor Burton-Edwards

DISCIPLESHIP
RESOURCES

ISBN: 978-0-88177-941-7

A DISCIPLE'S JOURNAL—YEAR B: A Guide for Daily Prayer, Bible Reading, and Discipleship. Copyright © 2020 Discipleship Resources®, Nashville, Tennessee. All rights reserved. No part of this book may be reproduced in any form whatsoever, print or electronic, without written permission. For information regarding rights and permissions, contact Discipleship Resources®, 1908 Grand Avenue, Nashville, TN 37212.

Discipleship Resources® is an imprint of Upper Room Books®. Discipleship Resources® and design logos are trademarks owned by The Upper Room®, Nashville, Tennessee. All rights reserved.

Discipleship Resources® web page: discipleshipresources.org

Upper Room Books® website: upperroombooks.com

Revised Common Lectionary Copyright © 1992 Consultation on Common Texts. Used by permission.

Scripture quotations, unless otherwise indicated, are from the New Revised Standard Version Bible. Copyright © 1989 Division of Christian Education of the National Council of Churches of Christ in the United States of America. Used by permission. All rights reserved.

Cover design by GoreStudio, Inc.
Interior by PerfecType, Nashville, TN

DR941

"O that we may all receive of Christ's fullness,
grace upon grace;
grace to pardon our sins, and subdue our iniquities;
to justify our persons and to sanctify our souls;
and to complete that holy change, that renewal of our hearts,
whereby we may be transformed
into that blessed image wherein thou didst create us."

✢ John Wesley ✦

Contents

Lent

Holy Week

Easter

The Season after Pentecost (Ordinary Time)

Wesleyan Discipleship

O that we could begin this day
in devout meditations,
in joy unspeakable,
and in blessing and praising thee,
who hast given us such good hope
and everlasting consolation.
Lift up our minds
above all these little things below,
which are apt to distract our thoughts;
and keep them above,
till our hearts are fully bent
to seek thee every day,
in the way wherein
Jesus hath gone before us,
though it should be with
the loss of all we here possess.

JOHN WESLEY
A Collection of Prayers for Families

How to Use *A Disciple's Journal*

John Wesley encouraged Christians to pray and read Scripture at the beginning and the end of every day. *A Disciple's Journal* is designed to help you habitually open your heart to grace by beginning and ending each day in the presence of the Triune God.

A Disciple's Journal contains two facing pages for each week of the year:

- **The left-hand page** is a guide for daily Bible reading with the Revised Common Lectionary Daily Readings.

  Sunday, the Lord's Day, is at the center. The lessons for Thursday, Friday, and Saturday prepare you for Sunday. The lessons for Monday, Tuesday, and Wednesday reflect upon Sunday.

  Lessons from the Old and New Testament are selected for each day of the week. The New Testament lessons for Saturday and Wednesday are from one of the Gospels.

  The lectionary includes two periods outside the seasons of Lent and Easter, Advent and Christmas called "Ordinary Time." The 33 or 34 Sundays that fall in the periods after the Baptism of the Lord and after Pentecost form a distinct sequence and are guided by the gospel of the year.

  The Sundays of Ordinary Time after Epiphany are designated by the number weeks after Epiphany, January 6. The length of this first Ordinary Time is determined by Ash Wednesday. Use the daily lectionary for Transfiguration Sunday for the week that includes Ash Wednesday.

  The Sundays of Ordinary Time after Pentecost are designated "Sunday between [Month] [Date] and [Date] inclusive." For example: "Sunday between May 24 and 28 inclusive."

  The bottom half of the page is divided into four quadrants that correspond to the General Rule of Discipleship (see pages 178–79). Use this space to record your acts of compassion, justice, worship, and devotion during the week.

- **The right-hand page** contains portions of hymns by Charles Wesley and excerpts from sermons by John Wesley, unless otherwise indicated. You will also find a prayer for each week based upon the Sunday scripture lessons. These prayers are written by members of the Consultation on Common Texts (www.commontexts.org). They are used here by permission.

If you are in a Covenant Discipleship group (see pages 180–82) or another type of small group, bring *A Disciple's Journal* to your weekly meeting. It will help you remember what you have done during the week. You may also record prayer concerns from the group.

The Daily Lectionary

A lectionary is a systematic way of reading the Bible guided by the church's liturgical calendar. It unites the global Church in prayer and worship. The daily lectionary used in *A Disciple's Journal* was developed by the Consultation on Common Texts (commontexts.org). It is used here by permission.

The Revised Common Lectionary (RCL) is organized as a three-year cycle. Each year emphasizes one of the Synoptic Gospels. Year B is shaped by the Gospel According to Mark, with significant portions of the Gospel According to John included during Lent and Easter. Because the RCL is intended for use in Sunday worship, it necessarily neglects significant portions of the Bible. The daily lectionary fills in the gaps.

Four Scripture lessons are selected for Sunday; two lessons from the Old Testament and two lessons from the New Testament. The first text is from the historical, wisdom, or prophetic books. The second is a Psalm that reflects a theme from the first lesson. The third lesson is from one of the epistles. And the final text is from one of the Gospels.

Prayer in the Morning and at Night

Pages 19 through 23 contain guides for daily prayer in the morning and at night. They are adapted from *The Book of Common Prayer*, which was the prayer book of John and Charles Wesley.

The collects for each day of the week are ancient prayers of the Church. Praying these simple guides of daily prayer with the collects is a way of joining your prayers with Christians around the world and throughout history.

The Psalm

Two psalms are appointed for most weeks. The first psalm is read with the lessons selected for Thursday, Friday, and Saturday. This psalm is also read, chanted, or sung in Sunday worship. The second psalm is read with the lessons assigned for Monday, Tuesday, and Wednesday.

Read the psalm to prepare your heart and mind before you read the other texts for the day. Reading the same psalm for several days helps you dwell in God's Word. Listen for what God is saying to you, the Church, and the world. Conclude the psalm by saying or singing the Gloria Patri

. . . the Gloria Patri::

**Glory to the Father, and to the Son, and to the Holy Spirit:
as it was in the beginning, is now, and will be forever. Amen.**

The Hymn

A Charles Wesley hymn is provided each week. Hymns are an important resource for Christian formation in the Wesleyan tradition. Like the Psalms, the hymn for the week may be either said or sung each day. Take time to reflect upon the words and allow them to open your heart to God and his grace. Let them become part of you. Memorize the hymn along with the Psalms.

A Cycle of Intercession

To help broaden your daily prayer "A Cycle of Intercession" is provided beginning on page 25. In the Lord's Prayer Jesus instructs us to pray "Your kingdom come, your will be done, on earth as in heaven." The cycle of intercessions encourages us to pray for the world each day.

A Blessing

I pray that *A Disciple's Journal* will be a blessing to you and your small group. If you are not in a small group for mutual accountability and support for growth in holiness of heart and life, I pray that you will find or form one.

> "Let us hold fast to the confession of our hope without wavering, for he who has promised is faithful. And let us consider how to provoke one another to love and good deeds, not neglecting to meet together, as is the habit of some, but encouraging one another, and all the more as you see the Day approaching" (Hebrews 10:23-25).

Rev. Steven W. Manskar, D. Min.
Pastor—Trinity United Methodist Church
Grand Rapids, Michigan
steven.manskar@gmail.com

Using *A Disciple's Journal* with Your Small Group

A Disciple's Journal is an excellent small group resource. The following are some examples of how the *Journal* may be used to help form disciples of Jesus Christ in small groups:

- Adopt the General Rule of Discipleship as your group's rule of life. Use the *Journal* to record how you have witnessed to Jesus Christ in the world and followed his teachings through acts of compassion, justice, worship, and devotion under the guidance of the Holy Spirit.
    - » The General Rule provides the agenda when the group meets.
    - » Begin with a prayer, read one of the Scripture lessons for the day, ask "What is God saying to us in this lesson today?"
    - » The leader then asks each person in turn, beginning with himself or herself, "How does your soul prosper?" The General Rule of Discipleship guides each person as they respond to the question.
    - » The group prays for each person after they've shared their response.
    - » The meeting concludes with singing a hymn, sharing prayer concerns, and praying the prayer for the week from *A Disciple's Journal.*
    - » Quarterly identify a specific area of the General Rule each person, or the group, wants to focus and grow; review the group's prayer concerns and goals.
- Advent, Lenten, and Easter study groups read the Scripture lessons for each day of the season and discuss the various themes, ideas, and images that emerge when they meet. Pray the prayer for each week along with the recommendations in the Cycle of Intercession.
- Groups may read and discuss the excerpts from John Wesley's sermon provided for that week.
- Read, reflect, and discuss the hymns of Charles Wesley. His poetry is a rich resource for study, theological reflection, and prayer.

Using *A Disciple's Journal* as a Family

Melanie C. Gordon

Ye that are truly kind parents, in the morning, in the evening, and all the day beside, press upon all your children, "to walk in love, as Christ also loved us, and gave himself for us;" to mind that one point, "God is love; and he that dwelleth in love, dwelleth in God, and God in him."
—John Wesley, *On the Education of Children*

John Wesley was committed to the education and formation of children. In his sermons, *On the Education of Children* and *On Family Religion*, Wesley emphasizes children's holiness and fitness for eternal joy with God; and the important role of parents in helping their children "walk in love". Praying together as a family is a tradition in Christian households. When we pray as a family, we connect with one another in a way that deepens intimacy with one another and with God. Whether we gather around the kitchen table, in the family room, or via technology when our families cannot be physically present with one another, daily prayer as a family offers the opportunity to grow in faith as children of God. The Gospels are clear that we are to make the way clear for children to discover Jesus. This is imperative in the church community, and in our homes where parents are the first and most significant teachers of their children. The home should be considered a sacred shelter, a place where "unconditional love, affirmation, challenges to accountability, and forgiveness are known; to learn and share rituals, symbols, and stories of faith; to recognize and claim their special gifts and mission in the world" (*Family the Forming Center*, Marjorie Thompson, p. 144).

As the world pulls parents in many directions, finding intentional time with our families can be challenging. Scripture tells us to teach children the words of God, "Recite them to your children. Talk about them when you are sitting around your house and when you are out and about, when you are lying down and when you are getting up" (Deuteronomy 6:7). Taking time to engage with one another and the world daily, strengthened by the love of God, is most effective when done in a pattern of time and rhythm. Family rituals create a sense of belonging, allowing each member to understand what is important in the family and offering a sense of identity. Rituals provide rhythm and consistency to our lives, allowing us to move spiritually from one place to another. Through ritual comes healing, connection and growth. What is realistic for a family that needs to get children up, dressed, fed, and off to school? What is realistic for families whose children are involved in activities after school, homework followed by dinner and bedtime? Each family has its own rhythm, and this guide is designed for families to create a rhythm in their life that intentionally includes time for family prayer, scripture and discipleship. Look at this as not just one more thing to put on an already hectic schedule. See this as a way to grow closer to God as a family, thereby helping children to engage in the world equipped as representatives of God in the world.

Setting the Space

Create a holy space or sacred space within the home. This can be as simple as a corner in the family room that contains symbols of faith—a candle, a cross, a small container of water, a cup, prayer beads, and a children's Bible. Take some time to ask your children what they think of when they think of God's love, and search the house for symbols that represent this.

Prayer boxes provide a concrete and safe place for children to share their prayers with God. Not all of us are comfortable praying aloud, and some children so not possess the language to share what is on their hearts. Writing or drawing their prayers offers children a way to release what they are feeling and hold on to these feelings while sharing them with God.

Prayer beads allow for a tangible way for children to relate to God. There are several ways to use prayer beads. Each bead can represent a prayer for a specific person or situation, beads can be held in the hand as a reminder of our connection with God, or beads can be used as the Israelites held fringe in their hands to remember that God will never abandon them.

Candles are a way to remind children that God is with us. Light a candle as you begin your daily prayers as a symbol that Christ is the light of the world. Encourage children to carefully blow out the candle at the end of your family prayers to symbolize taking the light out into the world as representatives of Christ in the world.

During Daily Prayers

Sharing scripture with children of different ages can be a challenge, and the Bible reading assigned for each day may be a bit overwhelming for children to sit through each day. Read the scripture ahead of time. Use a bible translation that children will connect with. After you read the scripture, simply share the narrative with your children in a way that you know they will understand.

Bless your children each day, as they are each a blessing from God who need to hear that on a regular basis. After daily prayers, take a moment and get on the physical level of each child, look each child in the eye, and with your thumb or pointing finger make the sign of the cross on their forehead and say, "you are a blessing." Children love being reminded that they are blessings in our lives.

Extending Daily Prayers

Three ways to use the Jerusalem cross as a visual reminder for children:

- **Make a copy** of the Jerusalem cross to place on the refrigerator or a central place in your home as a reminder for children of how we love God and offer God's love to others.
- **Let children draw a copy** of the Jerusalem cross, and then encourage them to draw or write how they have lived into works of piety and mercy each week.
- Since we live in a culture where we are often on-the-go, **keep a copy** of the Jerusalem cross in the car as a conversation starter for children to share how they have experienced acts of worship, justice, devotion, and compassion.

Taking the Light of God into the World

Serve the community as a family. Balancing our works of piety with works of mercy will allow us, and our children live into the command to love God and neighbor. Use the Jerusalem cross as a guide to help children find ways that you can serve others through acts of compassion and justice.

Children notice the world around them with awe and wonder, offering adults the opportunity to appreciate the world through their eyes if we only take the time to listen. Use time in the car, on the bus, or on the train to ask them what they noticed today that reminded them of something from morning prayer. They may need a little prompting, so ask them what they noticed during the day. You may also want to ask them what they wondered about today.

Guides for Family Prayer

PRAYER IN THE MORNING

Call to Prayer

The Call to Prayer in A Disciple's Journal *is quite appropriate for family daily prayer.*

Scripture

Choose one text to share from an age-appropriate translation of the Bible.

Silence

Keep the time for silent reflection appropriate for the ages of your children. As you practice as a family, the silence will become more focused and comfortable for the children.

Hymn

There are a couple of options for hymn singing. Recite or sing the hymn together, and ask the children which words stand out for them. You may also want to choose a hymn that they enjoy singing and make it a regular morning hymn.

Prayers for Ourselves and Others

Offer children the space to share their prayers. You may want to teach them the response, "Lord, hear our prayer" following each prayer.

The Lord's Prayer

The Collect

Use the list of Collects for Families appointed for each day. If your children are readers, and feel comfortable, allow them to take turns reading the Collects.

Blessing

Make the sign of the cross on each child's forehead and say, "As you go through your day, remember that you are a blessing" *or* "You are a blessing" *or* "Remember that you are a blessing."

Collects for Morning Prayer

SUNDAY

Almighty God, you are the source of all that is glorious. Fill our hearts with your gladness today, and in all we do today, help us worship you with gladness, through Jesus Christ and in the Holy Spirit. Amen.

MONDAY

All-knowing God, you offer great guidance for us each day. Open our hearts and minds that we will follow you joyfully through the challenges of the day, through Jesus Christ and in the Holy Spirit. Amen.

TUESDAY

God of peace, you sent Jesus as the Prince of Peace. Open our hearts that we will offer peace to people we encounter today, through Jesus Christ and in the Holy Spirit. Amen.

WEDNESDAY

God of grace, you offer us grace that we do not always deserve. As we encounter people today, help us to remember and extend grace to them, through Jesus Christ and in the Holy Spirit. Amen.

THURSDAY

Most Holy God, you are the greatest guide we will ever have in our lives. As we go about our day today, help us to remember that you will guide us through any challenges today, through Jesus Christ and in the Holy Spirit. Amen.

FRIDAY

Most Holy God, you created a world filled with mystery and wonder. In all we do today, help us to notice the beauty of this world, through Jesus Christ and in the Holy Spirit. Amen.

SATURDAY

Lord God, you gave us a world to care for and serve. As we go through this day, help us the notice and respond to ways we can serve you, through Jesus Christ and in the Holy Spirit. Amen.

PRAYER AT NIGHT

Call to Prayer

The Call to Prayer for Night Prayer in A Disciple's Journal *(page 22) is quite appropriate for family daily prayer.*

Scripture

Reread the scripture text that you and your family shared during morning prayer. Offer children an opportunity to share what they notice about the scripture reading.

Prayers for Ourselves and Others

Offer children the space to share their prayers. You may want to teach them the response, "Lord, hear our prayer" following each prayer.

The Lord's Prayer

The Collect

Use the same Collect for Evening each night to conclude the day with something that is familiar and offers security.

Blessing

Make the sign of the cross on each child's forehead and say, "As you go to sleep tonight, remember that you are a blessing" *or* "You are a blessing" *or* "Remember that you are a blessing."

Collect for Evening

Lord, Jesus Christ, you made this day,
> and surrounded our work and play with your love all day.

Thank you for watching over us,
> and bringing us together tonight as a family of God.

Bless and watch over us through the night. Amen.

Find a list of Bibles and books for children at http://bit.ly/2o0gEjG

Family Prayer While Traveling

Our work and responsibilities outside of the home can take us away from our families for periods of time. **When you cannot be with your children**, adapt the daily prayers and Bible reading to share over the telephone or video technology to keep you connected to one another and God. To stay connected, let your children choose a symbol of faith that you can take with you on your trip. Plan a time for each morning and evening to connect. Use the Jerusalem Cross to share ways that each person offered compassion or addressed a social issue. This will open conversation about joys and sorrows of the day. Continue with a prayer followed by the Lord's Prayer, the Collect for Families, and a blessing for your child(ren).

When you travel as a family, let the children choose a symbol or symbols to carry with you. Plan a time for the family connect each morning and evening that you are away. Ideally, continue the same family ritual of daily prayers. If this is not possible, choose a space to gather as a family. Use the Jerusalem Cross to share ways that each person offered compassion or addressed a social issue. Begin with a prayer followed by the Lord's Prayer, the Collect for Families, and a blessing for your child(ren). This will continue the consistency and rhythm that children need to feel loved and secure.

Prayer in the Morning and at Night

A Cycle of Intercession

Morning Prayer

CALL TO PRAYER (from Psalm 51)
>Open my lips, O Lord,
>>and my mouth shall proclaim your praise.
>
>Create in me a clean heart, O God,
>>and renew a right spirit within me.
>
>Glory to the Father, and to the Son, and to the Holy Spirit:
>>as it was in the beginning, is now, and will be forever. Amen.

SCRIPTURE   *The Psalm and one, or both, of the lessons for the day are read.*

SILENCE   *What captured your imagination?*
>*What is God up to in this text for your mission today?*

HYMN   *The hymn for the week may be said or sung;*
>*the Apostles' Creed (see page 24) may be said.*

PRAYERS FOR OURSELVES AND FOR OTHERS
>*See* A Cycle of Intercession *on pages 25–27.*

THE LORD'S PRAYER
>Our Father in heaven, hallowed be your Name,
>>your kingdom come,
>>your will be done, on earth as in heaven.
>
>Give us today our daily bread.
>Forgive us our sins
>>as we forgive those who sin against us.
>
>Save us from the time of trial,
>>and deliver us from evil.
>
>For the kingdom, the power,
>>and the glory are yours,
>>now and for ever. Amen.

THE PRAYERS   *The collect for the day of the week (see page 21) and/or the Prayer for the week is said.*

Collects for the Morning

SUNDAY

O God, you make us glad with the weekly remembrance of the glorious resurrection of your Son our Lord: Give us this day such blessing through our worship of you, that the week to come may be spent in your favor; through Jesus Christ our Lord. Amen.

MONDAY (*for Renewal of Life*)

O God, the King eternal, whose light divides the day from the night and turns the shadow of death into the morning: Drive far from us all wrong desires, incline our hearts to keep your law, and guide our feet into the way of peace; that, having done your will with cheerfulness during the day, we may, when night comes, rejoice to give you thanks; through Jesus Christ our Lord. Amen.

TUESDAY (*for Peace*)

O God, the author of peace and lover of concord, to know you is eternal life and to serve you is perfect freedom: Defend us, your humble servants, in all assaults of our enemies; that we, surely trusting in your defense, may not fear the power of any adversaries; through the might of Jesus Christ our Lord. Amen.

WEDNESDAY (*for Grace*)

Lord God, almighty and everlasting Father, you have brought us in safety to this new day: Preserve us with your mighty power, that we may not fall into sin, nor be overcome by adversity; and in all we do, direct us to the fulfilling of your purpose; through Jesus Christ our Lord. Amen.

THURSDAY (*for Guidance*)

Heavenly Father, in you we live and move and have our being: We humbly pray you so to guide and govern us by your Holy Spirit, that in all the cares and occupations of our life we may not forget you, but may remember that we are ever walking in your sight; through Jesus Christ our Lord. Amen.

FRIDAY

Almighty God, whose most dear Son went not up to joy but first he suffered pain, and entered not into glory before he was crucified: Mercifully grant that we, walking in the way of the cross, may find it none other than the way of life and peace; through Jesus Christ your Son our Lord. Amen.

SATURDAY

Almighty God, who after the creation of the world rested from all your works and sanctified a day of rest for all your creatures: Grant that we, putting away all earthly anxieties, may be duly prepared for the service of your sanctuary, and that our rest here upon earth may be a preparation for the eternal rest promised to your people in heaven; through Jesus Christ our Lord. Amen.

Night Prayer

CALL TO PRAYER

O gracious Light,
    pure brightness of the everliving Father in heaven,
O Jesus Christ, holy and blessed!
Now as we come to the setting of the sun,
    and our eyes behold the evening light,
      we sing your praises, O God: Father, Son, and Holy Spirit.
You are worthy at all times to be praised by happy voices,
    O Son of God, O Giver of life,
and to be glorified through all the worlds.

SCRIPTURE   *The Psalm and one, or both, of the lessons for the day may be read.*

PRAYERS FOR OURSELVES AND FOR OTHERS

Recall and examine your day. When did you meet Christ?
When did you deny Christ? When did you serve Christ?

THE LORD'S PRAYER

Our Father in heaven, hallowed be your Name,
    your kingdom come,
    your will be done, on earth as in heaven.
Give us today our daily bread.
Forgive us our sins
    as we forgive those who sin against us.
Save us from the time of trial,
    and deliver us from evil.
For the kingdom, the power,
    and the glory are yours,
      now and for ever. Amen.

THE COLLECT   *The collect for the day of the week (see page 23) and/or the*
                Prayer for the week are said.

Collects for the Night

SUNDAY

Lord God, whose Son our Savior Jesus Christ triumphed over the powers of death and prepared for us our place in the new Jerusalem: Grant that we, who have this day given thanks for his resurrection, may praise you in that City of which he is the light, and where he lives and reigns for ever and ever. Amen.

MONDAY

Most holy God, the source of all good desires, all right judgments, and all just works: Give to us, your servants, that peace which the world cannot give, so that our minds may be fixed on the doing of your will, and that we, being delivered from the fear of all enemies, may live in peace and quietness; through the mercies of Christ Jesus our Savior. Amen.

TUESDAY

Be our light in the darkness, O Lord, and in your great mercy defend us from all perils and dangers of this night; for the love of your Son, our Savior Jesus Christ. Amen.

WEDNESDAY

O God, the life of all who live, the light of the faithful, the strength of those who labor, and the repose of the dead: We thank you for the blessings of the day that is past, and humbly ask for your protection through the coming night. Bring us in safety to the morning hours; through him who died and rose again for us, your Son our Savior Jesus Christ. Amen.

THURSDAY

Lord Jesus, stay with us, for evening is at hand and the day is past; be our companion in the way, kindle our hearts, and awaken hope, that we may know you as you are revealed in Scripture and the breaking of bread. Grant this for the sake of your love. Amen.

FRIDAY

Lord Jesus Christ, by your death you took away the sting of death: Grant to us your servants so to follow in faith where you have led the way, that we may at length fall asleep peacefully in you and wake up in your likeness; for your tender mercies' sake. Amen.

SATURDAY

O God, the source of eternal light: Shed forth your unending day upon us who watch for you, that our lips may praise you, our lives may bless you, and our worship tomorrow give you glory; through Jesus Christ our Lord. Amen.

The Apostles' Creed

I believe in God, the Father almighty,
    creator of heaven and earth;
I believe in Jesus Christ his only Son our Lord;
    who was conceived by the power of the Holy Spirit,
    and born of the Virgin Mary,
    He suffered under Pontius Pilate,
      was crucified, died, and was buried.
    He descended to the dead.
    On the third day he rose again.
    He ascended into heaven,
      and is seated at the right hand of the Father.
    He will come again to judge the living and the dead.
I believe in the Holy Spirit,
    the holy catholic church,
    the communion of saints,
    the forgiveness of sins,
    the resurrection of the body,
    and the life everlasting. Amen.

Wesley Covenant Prayer

I am no longer my own, but thine.
Put me to what thou wilt, rank me with whom thou wilt.
Put me to doing, put me to suffering.
Let me be employed by thee or laid aside for thee,
    exalted for thee or brought low for thee.
Let me be full, let me be empty.
Let me have all things, let me have nothing.
I freely and heartily yield all things
    to thy pleasure and disposal.
And now, O glorious and blessed God,
    Father, Son, and Holy Spirit,
    thou art mine, and I am thine. So be it.
And the covenant which I have made on earth,
    let it be ratified in heaven. Amen.

A Cycle of Intercession

Prayers may include the following concerns if it is desired to pray for different topics through the week and the seasons.

Every day
- In the morning: the day and its tasks; the world and its needs; the Church and her life
- In the evening: peace; individuals and their needs

In Ordinary Time

Sunday
- The universal Church
- Bishops, annual conferences, central conferences and all who lead the Church
- The leaders of the nations
- The natural world and the resources of the earth
- All who are in any kind of need

Monday
- The media and the arts
- Farming and fishing
- Commerce and industry
- Those whose work is unfulfilling, stressful or fraught with danger
- All who are unemployed

Tuesday
- All who are sick in body, mind or spirit
- Those in the midst of famine or disaster
- Victims of abuse and violence, intolerance and prejudice
- Those who are bereaved
- All who work in the medical and healing professions

Wednesday
- The social services
- All who work in the criminal justice system
- Victims and perpetrators of crime
- The work of aid agencies throughout the world
- Those living in poverty or under oppression

Thursday

- Local government and community leaders
- All who provide local services
- Those who work with young or elderly people
- Schools, colleges, and universities
- Emergency and rescue organizations

Friday

- The president of the United States, members of Congress, and the armed forces
- Peace and justice in the world
- Those who work for reconciliation
- All whose lives are devastated by war and civil strife
- Prisoners, refugees, and homeless people

Saturday

- Our homes, families, friends, and all whom we love
- Those whose time is spent caring for others
- Those who are close to death
- Those who have lost hope
- The worship of the Church

In Seasonal Time

Advent

- The Church, that she may be ready for the coming of Christ
- The leaders of the Church
- The nations, that they may be subject to the rule of God
- Those who are working for justice in the world
- The broken, that they may find God's healing

Christmas

- The Church, especially in places of conflict
- The Holy Land, for peace with justice and reconciliation
- Refugees and asylum seekers
- Homeless people
- Families with young children

Epiphany

- The unity of the Church
- The peace of the world

- The revelation of Christ to those from whom his glory is hidden
- All who travel

Lent

- Those preparing for baptism and confirmation
- Those serving through leadership
- Those looking for forgiveness
- Those misled by the false gods of this present age
- All who are hungry

Holy Week

- The persecuted Church
- The oppressed peoples of the world
- All who are lonely
- All who are near to death
- All who are facing loss

Easter

- The people of God, that they may proclaim the risen Lord
- God's creation, that the peoples of the earth may meet their responsibility to care
- Those in despair and darkness, that they may find the hope and light of Christ
- Those in fear of death, that they may find faith through the resurrection
- Prisoners and captives

Ascension until Pentecost

- Those who wait on God, that they may find renewal
- The earth, for productivity and for fruitful harvests
- All who are struggling with broken relationships

All Saints until Advent

- The saints on earth, that they may live as citizens of heaven
- All people, that they may hear and believe the word of God
- All who fear the winter months
- All political leaders, that they may imitate the righteous rule of Christ
- All who grieve or wait with the dying

O that we might heartily surrender our wills to thine;
that we may unchangeably cleave unto it,
with the greatest and most entire affection to all thy commands.
O that there may abide for ever in us
such a strong and powerful sense of thy mighty love
towards us in Christ Jesus,
as may constrain us freely and willingly to please thee,
in the constant exercise of righteousness and mercy,
temperance and charity, meekness and patience,
truth and fidelity;
together with such an humble, contented, and peaceable spirit,
as may adorn the religion of our Lord and Master.
Yea, let it ever be the joy of our hearts to be righteous,
as thou art righteous;
to be merciful, as thou, our heavenly Father, art merciful;
to be holy, as thou who hast called us art holy,
to be endued with thy divine wisdom,
and to resemble thee in faithfulness and truth.
O that the example of our blessed Savior
may be always dear unto us,
that we may cheerfully follow him in every holy temper,
and delight to do thy will, O God.
Let these desires, which thou hast given us,
never die or languish in our hearts,
but be kept always alive, always in their vigor and force,
by the perpetual inspirations of the Holy Ghost.

JOHN WESLEY
A Collection of Prayers for Families

A Disciple's Journal
Year B

Help us to build each other up.
Our little stock improve;
Increase our faith, confirm our hope,
And perfect us in love.

CHARLES WESLEY

The Christian Year

The Christian Year organizes the worship of the Church to help Christians rehearse the life and ministry of Jesus and to disciple others in his way. The Christian Year combines evangelism, teaching, worship, the formation of disciples and mission, and helps the church keep all of these vital elements of its life and ministry constantly before it.

Advent

Orientation to Ultimate Salvation

The Christian Year begins with the end in mind. Advent is the season for orienting Christians to our place within God's work of salvation of the cosmos. Advent focuses primarily on the fulfillment of all things in Jesus Christ. It begins by reminding us of the second advent (coming) of Christ, the final judgment, the resurrection of the dead, and new creation. We then spend two weeks with the prophet known as John the Baptizer whose ministry and preaching about the judgment and end of this current age laid the groundwork for the teaching and ministry of Jesus. The final Sunday of Advent brings us to events leading up to the birth of Jesus.

Advent starts to work in us like a funnel. The purpose of a funnel is to concentrate everything that can flow into it into a smaller outlet so everything can fit into a smaller space. Advent takes in all of history from the "top" and concentrates it and all its meanings on one person, Jesus Christ. It takes in all time, past and future, and moving backward in time, leads us to the incarnation of God in Jesus Christ. It takes in whole cosmos and its complete renewal and leads us to the confusing and messy, which is to say, very human circumstances surrounding the birth of Jesus. It challenges us to take in the infinitely vast and incomprehensible and to see, hear and feel how all of it flows out of the son of Mary.

But the aim of Advent is not to fill up our heads with grand ideas. Advent, like the age to come it proclaims again and again, is intended to do nothing less that call us to repent and live the good news that God's kingdom, which will complete all that Advent describes, has drawn near.

This is why Advent was initially designed as a secondary season for preparing persons for baptism. Just as those preparing for baptism during Lent would be baptized at Easter, so those preparing for baptism during Advent would be baptized during Christmas Season, primarily on Epiphany.

As you read and pray daily this Advent, allow the funnel to do its orienting and re-orienting work in you. But more than this, expect the Spirit's refilling, even now, to make all things new in you.

Rev. Taylor Burton-Edwards

First Sunday of Advent

Preparation for Sunday
Daily: Psalm 80:1-7, 17-19

Thursday
Zechariah 13:1-9
Revelation 14:6-13

Friday
Zechariah 14:1-9
1 Thessalonians 4:1-18

Saturday
Micah 2:1-13
Matthew 24:15-31.

Sunday
Isaiah 64:1-9
Psalm 80:1-7, 17-19
1 Corinthians 1:3-9
Mark 13:24-37

Reflection on Sunday
Daily: Psalm 79

Monday
Micah 4:1-5
Revelation 15:1-8

Tuesday
Micah 4:6-13
Revelation 18:1-10

Wednesday
Micah 5:1-5a
Luke 21:34-38

The General Rule of Discipleship
*To witness to Jesus Christ in the world and to follow his teachings
through acts of compassion, justice, worship, and devotion under the guidance of the Holy Spirit.*

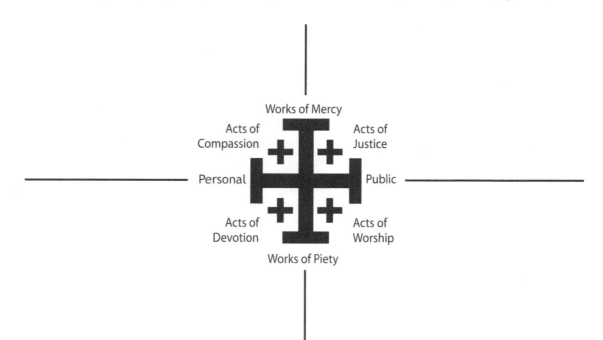

A Word from John Wesley

This is the original design of the Church of Christ. It is a body of men compacted together, in order, first, to save each his own soul; then to assist each other in working out their salvation; and, afterwards, as far as in them lies, to save all men from present and future misery, to overturn the kingdom of Satan, and set up the kingdom of Christ. And this ought to be the continued care and endeavour of every member of his Church; otherwise he is not worthy to be called a member thereof, as he is not a living member of Christ.

Sermon 52: "The Reformation of Manners," ¶ 2

A Hymn from Charles Wesley

Hearken to the solemn voice,
The awful midnight cry!
Waiting souls, rejoice, rejoice,
And see the bridegroom nigh!
Lo! he comes to keep his word;
Light and joy his looks impart;
Go ye forth to meet your Lord,
And meet him in your heart.

Wait we all in patient hope
Till Christ the Judge shall come;
We shall soon be all caught up
To meet the general doom;
In an hour to us unknown,
As a thief in deepest night,
Christ shall suddenly come down
With all his saints in light.

Happy he whom Christ shall find
Watching to see him come;
Him the Judge of all mankind
Shall bear triumphant home;
Who can answer to his word?
Which of you dares meet his day?
'Rise, and come to Judgment'—Lord,
We rise, and come away.
(*Collection—1781*, #53:1, 4 & 5)*

Prayers, Comments & Questions

Creator of the world, you are the potter, we are the clay, and you form us in your image. Shape our spirits by Christ's transforming power, that as one people we may live out your compassion and justice, whole and sound in the realm of your peace. Amen.

*Hymns labeled *Collection—1781* are from *A Collection of Hymns for the use of The People Called Methodists* published by John Wesley in 1781.

Second Sunday of Advent

Preparation for Sunday
Daily: Psalm 85:1-2, 8-13

Thursday
Hosea 6:1-6
1 Thessalonians 1:2-10

Friday
Jeremiah 1:4-10
Acts 11:19-26

Saturday
Ezekiel 36:24-28
Mark 11:27-33

Sunday
Isaiah 40:1-11
Psalm 85:1-2, 8-13
2 Peter 3:8-15a
Mark 1:1-8

Reflection on Sunday
Daily: Psalm 27

Monday
Isaiah 26:7-15
Acts 2:37-42

Tuesday
Isaiah 4:2-6
Acts 11:1-18

Wednesday
Malachi 2:10—3:1
Luke 1:5-17

The General Rule of Discipleship
*To witness to Jesus Christ in the world and to follow his teachings
through acts of compassion, justice, worship, and devotion under the guidance of the Holy Spirit.*

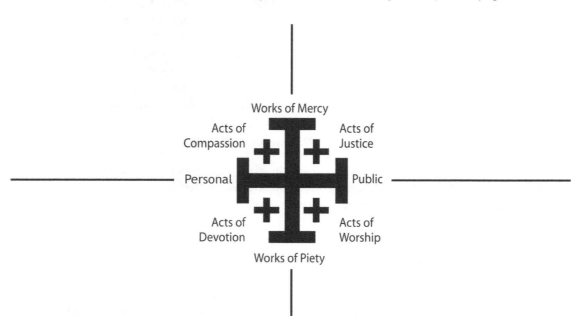

A Word from John Wesley

But if naked eternity, so to speak, be so vast, so astonishing an abject, as even to overwhelm your thought, how does it still enlarge the idea to behold it clothed with either happiness or misery! eternal bliss or pain! everlasting happiness, or everlasting misery! One would think it would swallow up every other thought in every reasonable creature. Allow me only this,—"Thou art on the brink of either a happy or miserable eternity; thy Creator bids thee now stretch out thy hand either to the one or the other;"—and one would imagine no rational creature could think on anything else. One would suppose that this single point would engross his whole attention. Certainly it ought so to do: Certainly, if these things are so, there can be but one thing needful. O let you and I, at least, whatever others do, choose that better part which shall never be taken away from us!

Sermon 54: "On Eternity," ¶ 19

A Hymn from Charles Wesley

He comes! he comes! the Judge severe!
The seventh trumpet speaks him near;
His light'nings flash, his thunders roll;
How welcome to the faithful soul!

From heaven angelic voices sound,
See the almighty Jesus crowned!
Girt with omnipotence and grace,
And glory decks the Saviour's face!

Descending on his azure throne,
He claims the kingdoms for his own;
The kingdoms all obey his word,
And hail him their triumphant Lord!

Shout all the people of the sky,
And all the saints of the Most High;
Our Lord, who now his right obtains,
For ever and for ever reigns.

(*Collection—1781*, #55)

Prayers, Comments & Questions

God of hope, you call us from the exile of sin with the good news of restoration; you build a highway through the wilderness; you come to us and bring us home. Comfort us with the expectation of your saving power, made known to us in Jesus Christ our Lord. Amen.

Third Sunday of Advent

Preparation for Sunday
Daily: Psalm 126

Thursday
Habakkuk 2:1-5
Philippians 3:7-11

Friday
Habakkuk 3:2-6
Philippians 3:12-16

Saturday
Habakkuk 3:13-19
Matthew 21:28-32

Sunday
Isaiah 61:1-4, 8-11
Psalm 126 *or*
    Luke 1:46b-55
1 Thessalonians 5:16-24
John 1:6-8, 19-28

Reflection on Sunday
Daily: Psalm 125

Monday
1 Kings 18:1-18
Ephesians 6:10-17

Tuesday
2 Kings 2:9-22
Acts 3:17—4:4

Wednesday
Malachi 3:16—4:6
Mark 9:9-13

The General Rule of Discipleship
To witness to Jesus Christ in the world and to follow his teachings
through acts of compassion, justice, worship, and devotion under the guidance of the Holy Spirit.

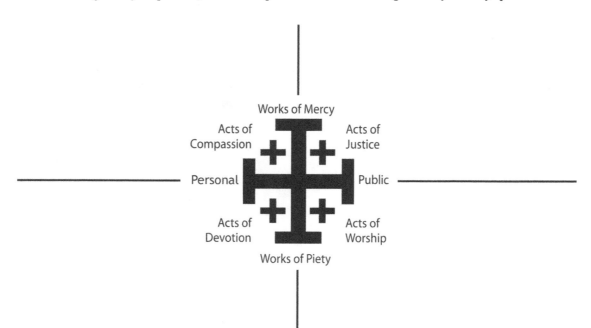

A Word from John Wesley

There are three that bear record in heaven: And these three are One. I believe this fact also, (if I may use the expression,) that God is Three and One. But the manner how I do not comprehend and I do not believe it. Now in this, in the manner, lies the mystery; and so it may; I have no concern with it: It is no object of my faith: I believe just so much as God has revealed, and no more. But this, the manner, he has not revealed; therefore, I believe nothing about it. But would it not be absurd in me to deny the fact, because I do not understand the manner That is, to reject what God has revealed, because I do not comprehend what he has not revealed.

Sermon 55: "On the Trinity," ¶ 15

A Hymn from Charles Wesley

Ye virgin souls arise,
With all the dead awake.
Unto salvation wise,
Oil in your vessels take:
Upstarting at the midnight cry,
Behold the heavenly bridegroom nigh.

He comes, he comes to call
The nations to his bar,
And raise to glory all
Who fit for glory are;
Made ready for your full reward,
Go forth with joy to meet your Lord.

Then let us wait to hear
The trumpet's welcome sound,
To see our Lord appear,
Watching let us be found;
When Jesus doth the heavens bow,
Be found—as, Lord, thou find'st us now!

(*Collection—1781*, #64:1, 2, & 6)

Prayers, Comments & Questions

Merciful God of peace, your word, spoken by the prophets, restores your people's life and hope. Fill our hearts with the joy of your saving grace, that we may hold fast to your great goodness and in our lives proclaim your justice in all the world. Amen.

Fourth Sunday of Advent

Preparation for Sunday
Daily: Psalm 89:1-4, 19-26

Thursday
2 Samuel 6:1-11
Hebrews 1:1-4

Friday
2 Samuel 6:12-19
Hebrews 1:5-14

Saturday
Judges 13:2-24
John 7:40-52

Sunday
2 Samuel 7:1-11, 16
Luke 1:46b-55 *or*
    Psalm 89:1-4, 19-26
Romans 16:25-27
Luke 1:26-38

Reflection on Sunday
Daily: Luke 1:46b-55

Monday
1 Samuel 1:1-18
Hebrews 9:1-14

Tuesday
1 Samuel 1:19-28
Hebrews 8:1-13

Wednesday
1 Samuel 2:1-10
Mark 11:1-11

The General Rule of Discipleship
To witness to Jesus Christ in the world and to follow his teachings
through acts of compassion, justice, worship, and devotion under the guidance of the Holy Spirit.

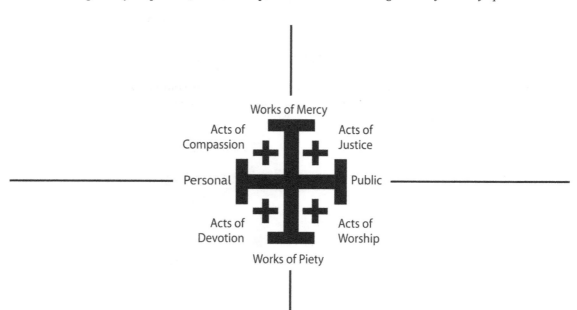

A Word from John Wesley

When God created the heavens and the earth, and all that is therein, at the conclusion of each day's work it is said, "And God saw that it was good." Whatever was created was good in its kind; suited to the end for which it was designed; adapted to promote the good of the whole and the glory of the great Creator. This sentence it pleased God to pass with regard to each particular creature. But there is a remarkable variation of the expression, with regard to all the parts of the universe, taken in connection with each other, and constituting one system: "And God saw everything that he had made, and, behold, it was very good."

Sermon 56: God's Approbation of His Work, ¶ 1

A Hymn from Charles Wesley

Father our hearts we lift,
Up to thy gracious throne,
And bless thee for the precious gift,
Of thine incarnate Son:
The gift unspeakable,
We thankfully receive,
And to the world thy goodness tell,
And to thy glory live.

Jesus the holy child,
Doth by his birth declare,
That God and man are reconciled,
And one in him we are:
Salvation through his name
To all mankind is given,
And loud his infant cries proclaim,
A peace 'twixt earth and heaven.

(*Hymns for the Nativity of Our Lord*—1745, #9:1 & 2)

Prayers, Comments & Questions

Ever-faithful God, through prophets and angels you promised to raise up a holy child who would establish a household of peace and justice. Open our hearts to receive your Son, that we may open our doors to welcome all people as sisters and brothers and establish your household in our time. Amen.

Christmas Season

The Aftermath of Incarnation

After Advent has "funneled" the cosmos into a Palestinian feed bin, Christmas Season opens up for us the global effects of the Word made flesh. Christmas Season is twelve days, starting with the Eve of Christmas, for the church to begin to unpack and wonder anew at all even the birth itself began to unleash then and continues to set loose now.

The readings for Christmas Season are full of violence, danger, and, bookended around these stories, blessing. We start and end the season (Christmas Eve and Epiphany) with the joyous announcement of angels to shepherds and Magi interpreting the stars. Between them we encounter the violence of Herod, hear of the genocidal deaths of thousands of male infants, and follow the family of Jesus on a desperate journey into Egypt not unlike the family of Jacob and their offspring had made. We remember the first Christian martyr, the deacon Stephen. We hear of Jesus' circumcision, and are reminded of the poverty of his family when we learn the sacrificial animals they could purchase for the rite of purification for Mary were those reserved for the poor.

All of these stories, and others we recount from the Bible, are there to keep us mindful that the kingdoms of this world do not welcome the coming of the kingdom of God, but violently resist it. They bear daily witness to the reading from John's gospel for Christmas Day. "He came to his own, and his own did not receive him." This is why we take the time to prepare persons and sponsors for baptism and discipleship. The world as we know it is not set up to receive our witness to Jesus. Indeed, it sets up myriad ways to put our witness to a violent and, from its angle at least, a shameful end.

But in and through all of these stories of opposition, we also remember the earlier words of our reading from Christmas Day. "The light shines in the darkness. And the darkness has not overcome it." And we are called to rehearse through these days, especially if we are accompanying candidates and sponsors toward baptism, that what we are given in Jesus is nothing less than to become, like him, children of God born not of our own striving, but by the will of God through water and the Holy Spirit.

Rev. Taylor Burton-Edwards

Days around Christmas Day

Daily
Psalm 96

December 22
Zephaniah 3:8-13
Romans 10:5-13

December 23
Zephaniah 3:14-20
Romans 13:11-14

December 24
(Morning)
Ecclesiastes 3:1-8
James 1:17-18

Christmas Day
Isaiah 9:2-7
Psalm 96
Titus 2:11-14
Luke 2:1-20

First Sunday after Christmas Day
Isaiah 61:10—62:3
Psalm 148
Galatians 4:4-7
Luke 2:22-40

Daily
Psalm 148

December 26
Jeremiah 26:1-9, 12-15
Acts 6:8-15; 7:51-60

December 27
Exodus 33:18-23
1 John 1:1-9

December 28
Jeremiah 31:15-17
Matthew 2:13-18

The General Rule of Discipleship
*To witness to Jesus Christ in the world and to follow his teachings
through acts of compassion, justice, worship, and devotion under the guidance of the Holy Spirit.*

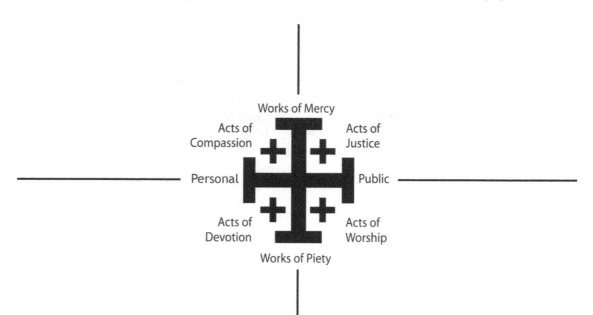

A Word from John Wesley

The plain scriptural notion of justification is pardon, the forgiveness of sins. It is that act of God the Father whereby, for the sake of the propitiation made by the blood of his Son, he 'showeth forth his righteousness (or mercy) by the remission of the sins that are past'. . . . God will not inflict on that sinner what he deserved to suffer, because the Son of his love hath suffered for him. And from the time we are 'accepted through the Beloved', 'reconciled to God through his blood', he loves and blesses and watches over us for good, even as if we had never sinned.

Sermon 5: Justification by Faith, § II.5

A Hymn from Charles Wesley

Glory be to God on high,
and peace on earth descend:
God comes down; he bows the sky,
and shews himself our friend!
God, the invisible, appears,
God, the blest, the great I AM,
Sojourns in this vale of tears,
and Jesus is his name.

Him the angels all adored.
Their maker and their King;
tidings of their humbled Lord,
they now to mortals bring;
emptied of his majesty,
of his dazzling glories shorn,
being's source begins to be,
and God himself is born!

(*Hymns for the Nativity of Our Lord*-1745, #4:1 & 2)

Prayers, Comments & Questions

God of glory, you have given us a new name and robed us in salvation. May we like Anna find our home in your presence, and like Simeon recognize Jesus as the Christ, so that, in joy and thanksgiving at becoming your children, we may join with all creation to sing your praise. Amen.

O God of ancient blessing, your servant Mary pondered in her heart the treasured words spoken about her Son our Savior Jesus Christ. Prepare our hearts to receive his Spirit, that our tongues may confess him Lord. Amen.

Days of Christmas

Daily
Psalm 148

December 29
Isaiah 49:5-15
Matthew 12:46-50

December 30
Proverbs 9:1-12
2 Peter 3:8-13

December 31
1 Kings 3:5-14
John 8:12-19

January 1
New Year's Day
Ecclesiastes 3:1-13
Psalm 8
Revelation 21:1-6a
Matthew 25:31-46

Holy Name of Jesus
Numbers 6:22-27
Psalm 8
Galatians 4:4-7
  or Philippians 2:5-11
Luke 2:15-21

Daily
Psalm 110

January 2
Proverbs 1:1-7
James 3:13-18

Second Sunday after Christmas, *January 2–5*
Jeremiah 31:7-14
Psalm 147:12-20
Ephesians 1:3-14
John 1:1-18

The General Rule of Discipleship
To witness to Jesus Christ in the world and to follow his teachings
through acts of compassion, justice, worship, and devotion under the guidance of the Holy Spirit.

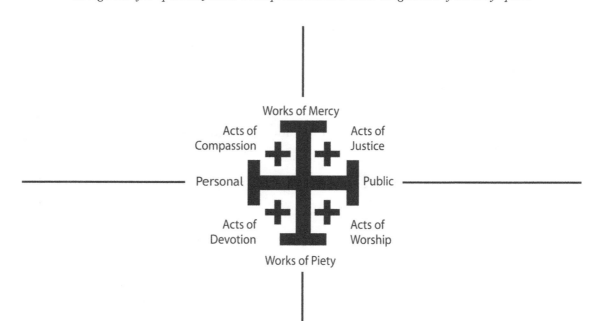

A Word from John Wesley

The plain scriptural notion of justification is pardon, the forgiveness of sins. It is that act of God the Father whereby, for the sake of the propitiation made by the blood of his Son, he 'showeth forth his righteousness (or mercy) by the remission of the sins that are past'. . . . God will not inflict on that sinner what he deserved to suffer, because the Son of his love hath suffered for him. And from the time we are 'accepted through the Beloved', 'reconciled to God through his blood', he loves and blesses and watches over us for good, even as if we had never sinned.

Sermon 5: Justification by Faith, § II.5

A Hymn from Charles Wesley

Glory be to God on high,
and peace on earth descend:
God comes down; he bows the sky,
and shews himself our friend!
God, the invisible, appears,
God, the blest, the great I AM,
Sojourns in this vale of tears,
and Jesus is his name.

Him the angels all adored.
Their maker and their King;
tidings of their humbled Lord,
they now to mortals bring;
emptied of his majesty,
of his dazzling glories shorn,
being's source begins to be,
and God himself is born!

(*Hymns for the Nativity of Our Lord*-1745, #4:1 & 2)

Prayers, Comments & Questions

God of new beginnings, you wipe away our tears and call us to care for one another. Give us eyes to see your gifts, hearts to embrace all creation, and hands to serve you every day of our lives. We ask this in the name of Jesus. Amen.

How majestic is your name in all the earth, O Lord our Sovereign! The heavens reflect your glory and the earth proclaims the wonder of your loving care. In the fulness of time you crowned creation with the birth of your Son. Continue your work of salvation among us and form us into a new creation that, as we behold the vision of a new heaven and a new earth, we may sing your glory. Amen.

Days around Epiphany

Readings through January 9 are provided for use if necessary. When the Epiphany of the Lord is transferred to the preceding Sunday, January 2-5, these dated readings may be used through the week that follows. When the Baptism of the Lord falls on January 11, 12, or 13, the corresponding preparation readings are used after January 9.

Daily
Psalm 110

January 3
Proverbs 1:20-33
James 4:1-10

January 4
Proverbs 3:1-12
James 4:11-17

January 5
Proverbs 22:1-9
Luke 6:27-31

January 6
Epiphany of the Lord
Isaiah 60:1-6
Psalm 72:1-7, 10-14
Ephesians 3:1-12
Matthew 2:1-12

Daily
Psalm 110

January 7
Exodus 1:22—2:10
Hebrews 11:23-26

January 8
Exodus 2:11-25
Hebrews 11:27-28

January 9
Exodus 3:7-15
John 8:39-59

The General Rule of Discipleship
*To witness to Jesus Christ in the world and to follow his teachings
through acts of compassion, justice, worship, and devotion under the guidance of the Holy Spirit.*

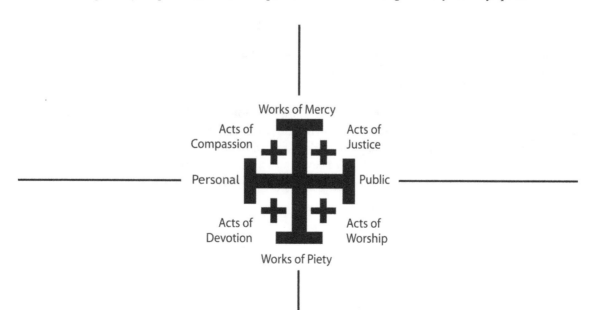

Works of Mercy

Acts of Compassion

Acts of Justice

Personal

Public

Acts of Devotion

Acts of Worship

Works of Piety

A Word from John Wesley

I am no longer my own, but thine.
Put me to what thou wilt,
    rank me with whom thou wilt. Put me to
doing, put me to suffering. Let me be employed
by thee or
laid aside for thee,
exalted for thee or
brought low for thee.
Let me be full, let me be empty.
Let me have all things,
let me have nothing.
I freely and heartily yield all things
    to thy pleasure and disposal.
And now, O glorious and blessed God, Father,
Son, and Holy Spirit,
    thou art mine, and I am thine.
So be it.
And the covenant
    which I have made on earth,
    let it be ratified in heaven.
Amen.

Wesleyan Covenant Prayer

A Hymn from Charles Wesley

Come, let us use the grace divine,
And all, with one accord,
In a perpetual covenant join
Ourselves to Christ the Lord.

Give up ourselves, through Jesu's power,
His name to glorify;
And promise, in this sacred hour,
For God to live and die.

The covenant we this moment make
Be ever kept in mind:
We will no more our God forsake,
Or cast his words behind.

To each the covenant blood apply,
Which takes our sins away;
And register our names on high,
And keep us to that day.

(*Short Hymns on Select Passages of Holy Scripture*-1762)

Prayers, Comments & Questions

Perfect Light of revelation, as you shone in the life of Jesus, whose epiphany we celebrate, so shine in us and through us, that we may become beacons of truth and compassion, enlightening all creation with deeds of justice and mercy. Amen.

The Season after Epiphany (Ordinary Time)

The Season of Evangelism

The Season after Epiphany is bookended by two celebrations: Baptism of the Lord, on the first Sunday after Epiphany and The Transfiguration of Jesus on the last Sunday, prior to Ash Wednesday. The sweep of these Sundays and the days between them prefigures the sweep of the Christian life, from justification and initiation (Baptism of the Lord) to entire sanctification (Transfiguration). While this season is of varying length because of the varying dates of Easter, and so the varying starting time for Ash Wednesday, its purpose is always to help the congregation "get ready to get ready." That is, this is the "introductory course," if you will, to the more intensive preparation for baptism and new commitments in discipleship Lent is designed to help the church undertake.

On the Sundays between Baptism of the Lord and Transfiguration, the Sunday readings from the Old Testament are chosen to correspond with the gospel readings, which cover the early ministry of Jesus and in particular his calling of disciples. The Old Testament and gospel readings thus particularly support the evangelistic work of the church reaching out to others during these weeks. The Epistle readings are not chosen to correspond with the other two, but rather to present a "semi-continuous" reading that will be picked up again during the Season after Pentecost. Though the Epistle readings do not directly connect to the gospel, they do still lay out basics of Christian life. One might say that the Epistle readings are there to evangelize the church by helping the church "get its own act together" as it prepares to accompany persons in intensive formation in the way of Jesus during Lent.

This gives individuals reading daily and worship leaders planning for weekly celebration two distinct paths they may follow during this season, either of which may contribute to this season's evangelistic purpose. As you undertake your readings through these weeks, you may wish to coordinate the attention you give to the daily readings based on the focus your worship leaders have chosen for Lord's Day worship to gain the maximum benefit from the correlation of the two.

Rev. Taylor Burton-Edwards

First Sunday after the Epiphany: *Baptism of the Lord*

Preparation for Sunday
Daily: Psalm 29

Thursday
1 Samuel 3:1-21
Acts 9:10-19a

Friday
1 Samuel 16:1-13
1 Timothy 4:11-16

Saturday,
1 Kings 2:1-4, 10-12
Luke 5:1-11

Sunday
Genesis 1:1-5
Psalm 29
Acts 19:1-7
Mark 1:4-11

Days around Epiphany
Daily: Psalm 69:1-5, 30-36

Monday
Genesis 17:1-13
Romans 4:1-12

Tuesday
Exodus 30:22-38
Acts 22:2-16

Wednesday
Isaiah 41:14-20
John 1:29-34

The General Rule of Discipleship
To witness to Jesus Christ in the world and to follow his teachings
through acts of compassion, justice, worship, and devotion under the guidance of the Holy Spirit.

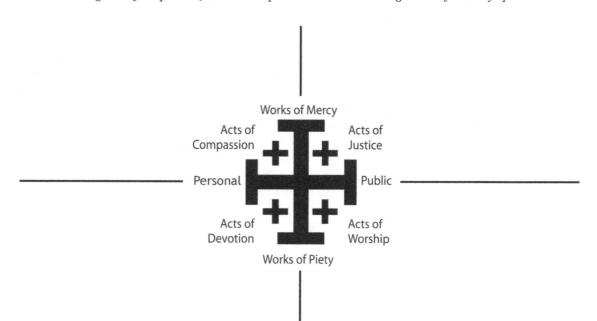

A Word from John Wesley

"That the Lord God might dwell in them:" This refers to a yet farther manifestation of the Son of God; even his inward manifestation of himself. When he spoke of this to his Apostles but a little before his death, one of them immediately asked, "Lord, how is it that thou wilt manifest thyself to us, and not unto the world?" By enabling us to believe in his name. For he is then inwardly manifested to us when we are enabled to say with confidence, "My Lord, and my God!" Then each of us can boldly say, "The life which I now live, I live by faith in the Son of God, who loved me and gave himself for me." [Gal. 2:20] And it is by thus manifesting himself in our hearts that he effectually "destroys the works of the devil."

Sermon 62: "The End of Christ's Coming," § II.7

A Hymn from Charles Wesley

Where is the holy heavenborn Child,
Heir of the everlasting Throne,
Who Heaven and Earth hath reconciled,
And God and man rejoined in one?

Shall we of earthly kings enquire,
To courts or palaces repair?
The nation's Hope, the world's Desire,
Alas! we cannot find Him there.

Shall learning show the sinner's Friend.
Or scribes a sight of Christ afford?
Us to his natal place they send,
But never go to see their Lord.

We search the outward Church in vain,
They cannot Him we seek declare,
They have not found the Son of Man,
Or known the sacred Name they bear.

Then let us turn no more aside,
But use the Light Himself imparts,
His Spirit is our surest Guide,
His Spirit glimmering in our hearts.

(*Hymns for the Nativity of Our Lord*—1745, #17:1-5)

Prayers, Comments & Questions

Holy God, creator of light and herald of goodness, at the waters of his baptism you proclaimed Jesus your beloved Son. With the baptized of every time and generation, may we say yes to your call to repentance and be led to the life of abundance we experience in your kinship and your love. Amen.

Second Sunday after the Epiphany

Preparation for Sunday
Daily: Psalm 139:1-6, 13-18

Thursday
Judges 2:6-15
2 Corinthians 10:1-11

Friday
Judges 2:16-23
Acts 13:16-25

Saturday
1 Samuel 2:21-25
Matthew 25:1-13

Sunday
1 Samuel 3:1-20
Psalm 139:1-6, 13-18
1 Corinthians 6:12-20
John 1:43-51

Reflection on Sunday
Daily: Psalm 86

Monday
1 Samuel 9:27—10:8
2 Corinthians 6:14—7:1

Tuesday
1 Samuel 15:10-31
Acts 5:1-11

Wednesday
Genesis 16:1-14
Luke 18:15-17

The General Rule of Discipleship
To witness to Jesus Christ in the world and to follow his teachings
through acts of compassion, justice, worship, and devotion under the guidance of the Holy Spirit.

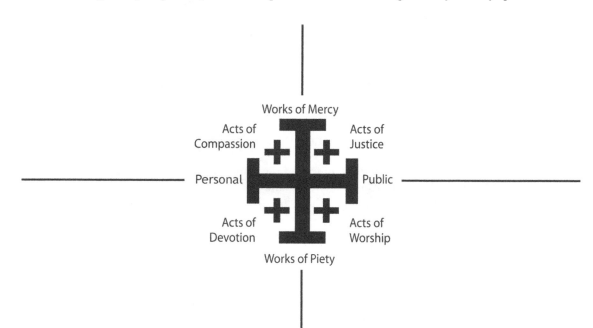

A Word from John Wesley

Yea, I am persuaded every child of God has had, at some time, "life and death set before him," eternal life and eternal death; and has in himself the casting voice. So true is that well-known saying of St. Austin, (one of the noblest he ever uttered,) *Qui fecit nos sine nobis, non salvabit nos sine nobis*: "He that made us without ourselves, will not save us without ourselves." Now in the same manner as God has converted so many to himself without destroying their liberty, he can undoubtedly convert whole nations, or the whole world; and it is as easy to him to convert a world, as one individual soul.

Sermon 63: The General Spread of the Gospel, ¶ 12.

A Hymn from Charles Wesley

Author of faith, eternal Word,
Whose Spirit breathes the active flame,
Faith, like its finisher and Lord,
Today as yesterday the same.

To thee our humble hearts aspire,
And ask the gift unspeakable:
Increase in us the kindled fire,
In us the work of faith fulfil.

By faith we know thee strong to save
(Save us, a present Saviour thou!)
Whate'er we hope, by faith we have,
Future and past subsisting now.

(*Collection—1781*, #92:1, 2, 3)

Prayers, Comments & Questions

Insistent God, by night and day you summon your slumbering people. So, stir us with your voice and enlighten our lives with your grace that we give ourselves fully to Christ's call to mission and ministry. Amen.

Third Sunday after the Epiphany

Preparation for Sunday
Daily: Psalm 62:5-12

Thursday
Jeremiah 19:1-15
Revelation 18:11-20

Friday
Jeremiah 20:7-13
2 Peter 3:1-7

Saturday
Jeremiah 20:14-18
Luke 10:13-16

Sunday
Jonah 3:1-5, 10
Psalm 62:5-12
1 Corinthians 7:29-31
Mark 1:14-20

Reflection on Sunday
Daily: Psalm 46

Monday
Genesis 12:1-9
1 Corinthians 7:17-24

Tuesday
Genesis 45:25—46:7
Acts 5:33-42

Wednesday
Proverbs 8:1-21
Mark 3:13-19a

The General Rule of Discipleship
To witness to Jesus Christ in the world and to follow his teachings
through acts of compassion, justice, worship, and devotion under the guidance of the Holy Spirit.

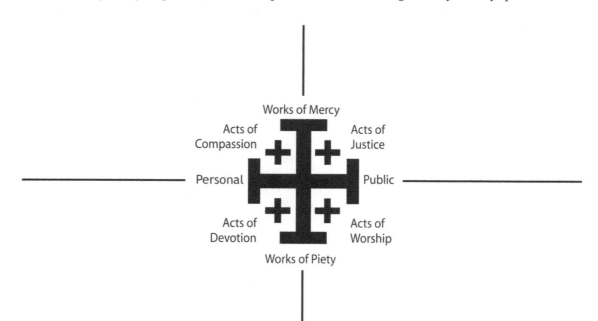

A Word from John Wesley

[God] is infinite in wisdom as well as in power: And all his wisdom is continually employed in managing all the affairs of his creation for the good of all his creatures. For his wisdom and goodness go hand in hand: They are inseparably united, and continually act in concert with Almighty power, for the real good of all his creatures. His power being equal to his wisdom and goodness, continually co-operates with them. And to him all things are possible: He doeth whatsoever pleaseth him, in heaven and earth, and in the sea, and all deep places: And we cannot doubt of his exerting all his power, as in sustaining, so in governing, all that he has made.

Sermon 67: "On Divine Providence" ¶ 14

A Hymn from Charles Wesley

To him that in thy name believes
Eternal life with thee is given;
Into himself he all receives—
Pardon, and holiness, and heaven.

The things unknown to feeble sense,
Unseen by reason's glimmering ray,
With strong commanding evidence
Their heavenly origin display.

Faith lends its realizing light,
The clouds disperse, the shadows fly;
Th'Invisible appears in sight,
And God is seen by mortal eye.

(*Collection—1781*, #92:4, 5, 6)

Prayers, Comments & Questions

God of the prophets, you call us from evil to serve you. Fulfill in us your commonwealth of justice and joy, that the light of your presence may be revealed to all nations to the glory of Jesus' name. Amen.

Fourth Sunday after the Epiphany

If this Sunday immediately precedes Ash Wednesday, the proper for Sunday and the readings for the surrounding days may be replaced, in those churches observing the Transfiguration on that Sunday, by the lessons for the Last Sunday after the Epiphany and the readings for the days surrounding it.

Preparation for Sunday
Daily: Psalm 111

Thursday
Deuteronomy 3:23-29
Romans 9:6-18

Friday
Deuteronomy 12:28-32
Revelation 2:12-17

Saturday
Deuteronomy 13:1-5
Matthew 8:28—9:1

Sunday
Deuteronomy 18:15-20
Psalm 111
1 Corinthians 8:1-13
Mark 1:21-28

Reflection on Sunday
Daily: Psalm 35:1-10

Monday
Numbers 22:1-21
Acts 21:17-26

Tuesday
Numbers 22:22-28
1 Corinthians 7:32-40

Wednesday
Jeremiah 29:1-14
Mark 5:1-20

The General Rule of Discipleship
*To witness to Jesus Christ in the world and to follow his teachings
through acts of compassion, justice, worship, and devotion under the guidance of the Holy Spirit.*

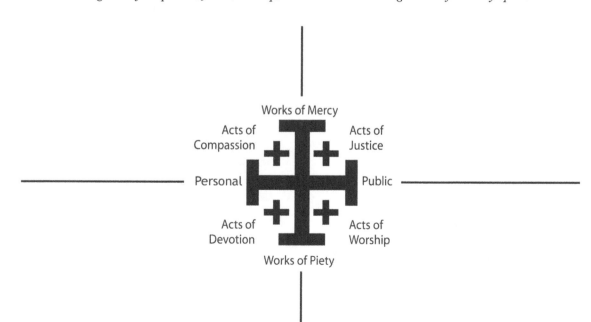

A Word from John Wesley

But have all that have sunk under manifold temptations, so fallen that they can rise no more Hath the Lord cast them all off for ever, and will he be no more entreated Is his promise come utterly to an end for evermore God forbid that we should affirm this! Surely He is able to heal all their backslidings: For with God no word is impossible. And is he not willing too He is "God, and not man; therefore his compassions fail not." Let no backslider despair. "Return unto the Lord, and he will have mercy upon you; unto our God, and he will abundantly pardon."

Sermon 68: "The Wisdom of God's Counsel," ¶ 24

A Hymn from Charles Wesley

How can a sinner know
His sins on earth forgiven?
How can my gracious Saviour show
My name inscribed in heaven?
What we have felt and seen
With confidence we tell,
And publish to the sons of men
The signs infallible.

We who in Christ believe,
That he for us hath died,
We all his unknown peace receive,
And feel his blood applied;
Exults our rising soul,
Disburdened of her load,
And swells unutterably full
Of glory and of God.

(Collection—1781, #93:1 & 2)

Prayers, Comments & Questions

Holy and awesome God, your Son's authority is found in integrity and living truth, not the assertion of power over others. Open our imaginations to new dimensions of your love, and heal us of all that severs us from you and one another, that we may grow into the vision you unfold before us. Amen.

Fifth Sunday after the Epiphany

If this Sunday immediately precedes Ash Wednesday, the proper for Sunday and the readings for the surrounding days may be replaced, in those churches observing the Transfiguration on that Sunday, by the lessons for the Last Sunday after the Epiphany and the readings for the days surrounding it.

Preparation for Sunday
Daily: Psalm 147:1-11, 20c

Thursday
Proverbs 12:10-21
Galatians 5:2-15

Friday
Job 36:1-23
1 Corinthians 9:1-16

Saturday
Isaiah 46:1-13
Matthew 12:9-14

Sunday
Isaiah 40:21-31
Psalm 147:1-11, 20c
1 Corinthians 9:16-23
Mark 1:29-39

Reflection on Sunday
Daily: Psalm 102:12-28

Monday
2 Kings 4:8-17, 32-37
Acts 14:1-7

Tuesday
2 Kings 8:1-6
Acts 15:36-41

Wednesday
Job 6:1-13
Mark 3:7-12

The General Rule of Discipleship
To witness to Jesus Christ in the world and to follow his teachings
through acts of compassion, justice, worship, and devotion under the guidance of the Holy Spirit.

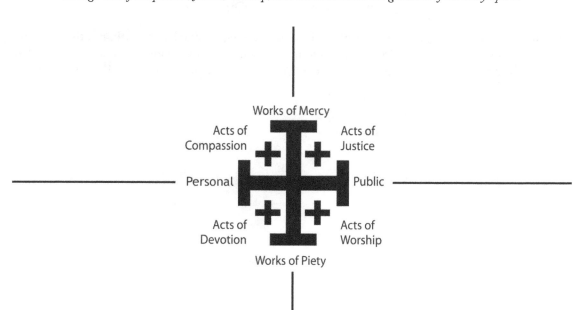

Works of Mercy

Acts of Compassion

Acts of Justice

Personal

Public

Acts of Devotion

Acts of Worship

Works of Piety

A Word from John Wesley

To begin with the great Creator himself. How astonishingly little do we know of God!—How small a part of his nature do we know! of his essential attributes! What conception can we form of his omnipresence Who is able to comprehend how God is in this and every place how he fills the immensity of space If philosophers, by denying the existence of a vacuum, only meant that there is no place empty of God, that every point of infinite space is full of God, certainly no man could call it in question. But still, the fact being admitted what is omnipresence or ubiquity Man is no more able to comprehend this, than to grasp the universe.

Sermon 69: "The Imperfection of Human Knowledge," § I.1

A Hymn from Charles Wesley

His love surpassing far
The love of all beneath,
We find within our hearts, and dare
The pointless darts of death.
Stronger than death or hell
The mystic power we prove;
And conqu'rors of the world, we dwell
In heaven, who dwell in love.

We by his Spirit prove
And know the things of God;
The things which freely of his love
He hath on us bestowed:
His Spirit to us he gave,
And dwells in us, we know;
The witness in ourselves we have,
And all his fruits we show.

(*Collection—1781*, #93:3 & 4)

Prayers, Comments & Questions

Everlasting God, you give strength to the powerless and power to the faint; you raise up the sick and cast out demons. Make us agents of healing and wholeness, that your good news may be made known to the ends of your creation. Amen.

Sixth Sunday after the Epiphany

If this Sunday immediately precedes Ash Wednesday, the proper for Sunday and the readings for the surrounding days may be replaced, in those churches observing the Transfiguration on that Sunday, by the lessons for the Last Sunday after the Epiphany and the readings for the days surrounding it.

Preparation for Sunday
Daily: Psalm 30

Thursday
Leviticus 13:1-17
Hebrews 12:7-13

Friday
Leviticus 14:1-20
Acts 19:11-20

Saturday
Leviticus 14:21-32
Matthew 26:6-13

Sunday
2 Kings 5:1-14
Psalm 30
1 Corinthians 9:24-27
Mark 1:40-45

Reflection on Sunday
Daily: Psalm 6

Monday
2 Chronicles 26:1-21
Acts 3:1-10

Tuesday
2 Kings 7:3-10
1 Corinthians 10:14—11:1

Wednesday
Job 30:16-31
John 4:46-54

The General Rule of Discipleship
To witness to Jesus Christ in the world and to follow his teachings
through acts of compassion, justice, worship, and devotion under the guidance of the Holy Spirit.

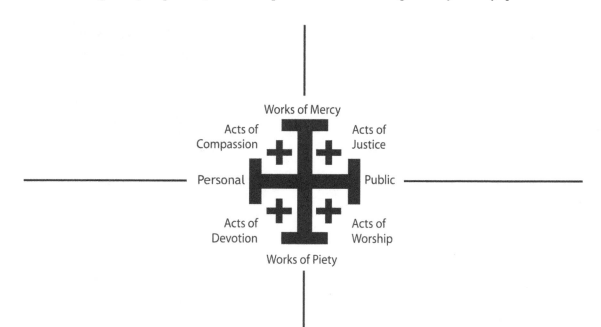

A Word from John Wesley

And, First, reason cannot produce faith. Although it is always consistent with reason, yet reason cannot produce faith, in the scriptural sense of the word. Faith, according to Scripture, is "an evidence," or conviction, "of things not seen." It is a divine evidence, bringing a full conviction of an invisible eternal world. It is true, there was a kind of shadowy persuasion of this, even among the wiser Heathens; probably from tradition, or from some gleams of light reflected from the Israelites. Hence many hundred years before our Lord was born, the Greek Poet uttered that great truth,—

Millions of spiritual creatures walk the earth
Unseen, whether we wake, or if we sleep.

But this was little more than faint conjecture: It was far from a firm conviction; which reason, in its highest state of improvement, could never produce in any child of man.

Sermon 70: "The Case of Reason Impartially Considered, §II.1

A Hymn from Charles Wesley

Gracious Redeemer, shake
This slumber from my soul!
Say to me now, Awake, awake
And Christ shall make thee whole.
Lay to thy mighty hand!
Alarm me in this hour,
And make me fully understand
The thunder of thy power!

Give me on thee to call,
Always to watch and pray,
Lest I into temptation fall,
And cast my shield away.
For each assault prepared
And ready may I be,
Forever standing on my guard,
And looking up to thee.

(*Collection—1781*, #296:1 & 2)

Prayers, Comments & Questions

Divine Physician, healer of bodies and souls, stretch out your hand and touch us. Cleanse our hearts from the sin that separates us from you and one another. Recreate us in your own image, and restore us in Christ, so that we may run the race and receive the prize of everlasting life. Amen.

Seventh Sunday after the Epiphany

If this Sunday immediately precedes Ash Wednesday, the proper for Sunday and the readings for the surrounding days may be replaced, in those churches observing the Transfiguration on that Sunday, by the lessons for the Last Sunday after the Epiphany and the readings for the days surrounding it.

Preparation for Sunday
Daily: Psalm 41

Thursday
2 Chronicles 7:12-23
3 John 2-8

Friday
Isaiah 38:1-8
Hebrews 12:7-13

Saturday
Isaiah 39:1-8
Luke 4:38-41

Sunday
Isaiah 43:18-25
Psalm 41
2 Corinthians 1:18-22
Mark 2:1-12

Reflection on Sunday
Daily: Psalm 38

Monday
Isaiah 30:18-26
Acts 14:8-18

Tuesday
Micah 4:1-7
2 Corinthians 1:1-11

Wednesday
Lamentation 5:1-22
John 5:19-29

The General Rule of Discipleship
To witness to Jesus Christ in the world and to follow his teachings
through acts of compassion, justice, worship, and devotion under the guidance of the Holy Spirit.

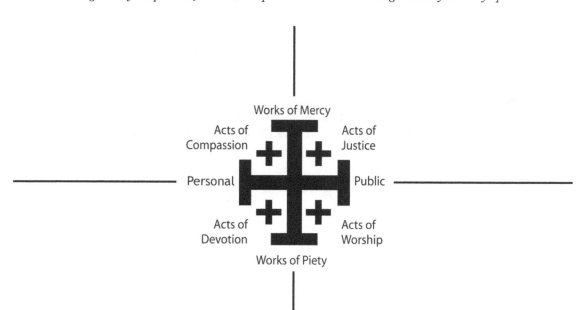

A Word from John Wesley

When a violent disease, supposed to be incurable, is totally and suddenly removed, it is by no means improbable that this is effected by the ministry of an angel. And perhaps it is owing to the same cause, that a remedy is unaccountably suggested either to the sick person, or some attending upon him, by which he is entirely cured.

Sermon 71: "On Good Angels," § II.4

A Hymn from Charles Wesley

O do thou always warn
My soul of evil near;
When to the right or left I turn,
The voice still let me hear:
'Com back! This is the way!
Come back, and walk herein!'
O may I hearken and obey,
And shun the paths of sin!

Thou seest my feebleness;
Jesu, be thou my power,
My help, and refuge in distress,
My fortress and my tower,
Give me to trust in thee,
Be thou my sure abode;
My horn, and rock, and buckler be,
My Saviour and my God.

(*Collection—1781*, #296:3 & 4)

Prayers, Comments & Questions

Faithful God, the fulfillment of your promise in Christ has brought new life to all creation: the forgiveness of sins and our restoration to wholeness. Anoint us with your Spirit, that we may be alert and mindful ministers of your gracious will to save, and persevere in bringing into your presence all that is broken and in need of healing, through Jesus Christ, our Lord. Amen.

Eighth Sunday after the Epiphany

If this Sunday immediately precedes Ash Wednesday, the proper for Sunday and the readings for the surrounding days may be replaced, in those churches observing the Transfiguration on that Sunday, by the lessons for the Last Sunday after the Epiphany and the readings for the days surrounding it.

Preparation for Sunday
Daily: Psalm 103:1-13, 22

Thursday
Ezekiel 16:1-14
Romans 3:1-8

Friday
Ezekiel 16:44-52
2 Peter 1:1-11

Saturday
Ezekiel 16:53-63
John 7:53—8:11

Sunday
Hosea 2:14-20
Psalm 103:1-13, 22
2 Corinthians 3:1-6
Mark 2:13-22

Reflection on Sunday
Daily: Psalm 45:6-17

Monday
Hosea 3:1-5
2 Corinthians 1:23—2:11

Tuesday
Hosea 14:1-9
2 Corinthians 11:1-15

Wednesday
Isaiah 62:1-5
John 3:22-36

The General Rule of Discipleship
To witness to Jesus Christ in the world and to follow his teachings
through acts of compassion, justice, worship, and devotion under the guidance of the Holy Spirit.

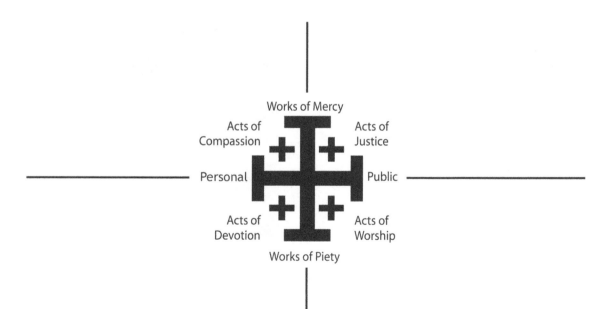

A Word from John Wesley

Next to the love of God, there is nothing which Satan so cordially abhors as the love of our neighbour. He uses, therefore, every possible means to prevent or destroy this; to excite either private or public suspicions, animosities, resentment, quarrels; to destroy the peace of families or of nations; and to banish unity and concord from the earth. And this, indeed, is the triumph of his art; to embitter the poor, miserable children of men against each other, and at length urge them to do his own work, to plunge one another into the pit of destruction.

Sermon 72: "On Evil Angels," § II.5

A Hymn from Charles Wesley

I want a principle within
Of jealous, godly fear,
A sensibility of sin,
A pain to feel it near.

That I from thee no more may part,
No more thy goodness grieve,
The filial awe, the fleshly heart,
The tender conscience give.

Quick as the apple of an eye,
O God, my conscience make;
Awake my soul when sin is nigh,
And keep it still awake.

If to the right or left I stray,
That moment, Lord, reprove,
And let me weep my life away
For having grieved thy love.

(*Collection—1781*, #299:1-4)

Prayers, Comments & Questions

Holy lover of Israel, hopeful spouse to a people, with tender words and covenant promise you invite us to meet your love with faithfulness. May we live with you in righteousness and justice, in steadfast love and mercy, to your glory forever. Amen.

Ninth Sunday after the Epiphany

The readings that follow are for churches whose calendar requires this Sunday and who do not observe the last Sunday after the Epiphany as Transfiguration.

Preparation for Sunday
Daily: Psalm 81:1-10

Thursday
Exodus 31:12-18
Acts 25:1-12

Friday
Leviticus 23:1-8
Romans 8:31-39

Saturday
Leviticus 24:5-9
John 7:19-24

Sunday
Deuteronomy 5:12-15
Psalm 81:1-10
2 Corinthians 4:5-12
Mark 2:23—3:6

Reflection on Sunday
Daily: Psalm 78:1-4, 52-72

Monday
Exodus 16:13-26
Romans 9:19-29

Tuesday
Exodus 16:27-36
Acts 15:1-5, 22-35

Wednesday
1 Samuel 21:1-6
John 5:1-18

The General Rule of Discipleship
To witness to Jesus Christ in the world and to follow his teachings
through acts of compassion, justice, worship, and devotion under the guidance of the Holy Spirit.

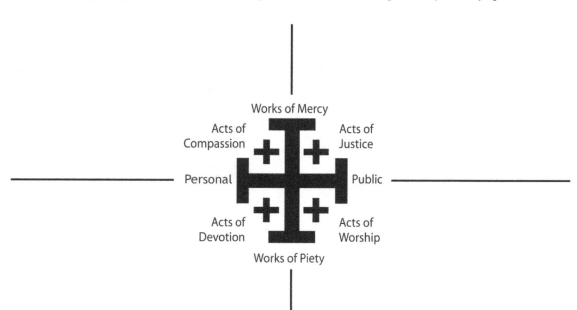

A Word from John Wesley

But as happy as the souls in paradise are, they are preparing for far greater happiness. For paradise is only the porch of heaven; and it is there the spirits of just men are made perfect. It is in heaven only that there is the fulness of joy; the pleasures that are at God's right hand for evermore. The loss of this, by those unhappy spirits, will be the completion of their misery. They will then know and feel, that God alone is the centre of all created spirits; and, consequently, that a spirit made for God can have no rest out of him. It seems that the Apostle had this in his view when he spoke of those "who shall be punished with everlasting destruction from the presence of the Lord." Banishment from the presence of the Lord is the very essence of destruction to a spirit that was made for God. And if that banishment lasts for ever, it is "everlasting destruction."

Sermon 73: "On Hell," § I.4

A Hymn from Charles Wesley

Jesu, my Saviour, Brother, Friend,
On whom I cast my every care,
On whom for all things I depend,
Inspire, and then accept my prayer.

If I have tasted of thy grace,
The grace that sure salvation brings,
If with me now thy Spirit stays,
And hovering hides me in this wings.

Still let him with my weakness stay,
Nor for a moment's space depart;
Evil and danger turn away,
And keep, till he renews my heart.

When to the right or left I stray,
His voice behind me may I hear:
'Return, and walk in Christ thy way;
Fly back to Christ; for sin is near.'

His sacred unction from above
Be still my comforter and guide,
Till all the stony he remove,
And in my loving heart reside.

(*Collection—1781*, #303:1-5)

Prayers, Comments & Questions

On this day of rest and gladness, we praise you, God of creation, for the dignity of work and the joy of play, for the challenge of witness and the invitation to delight at your table. Renew our hearts through your sabbath rest, that we might be refreshed to continue in your work of restoring the world to wholeness. Amen.

Last Sunday after the Epiphany: *Transfiguration Sunday*

Preparation for Sunday
Daily: Psalm 50:1-6

Thursday
1 Kings 11:26-40
2 Corinthians 2:12-17

Friday
1 Kings 14:1-18
1 Timothy 1:12-20

Saturday
1 Kings 16:1-7
Luke 19:41-44

Sunday
2 Kings 2:1-12
Psalm 50:1-6
2 Corinthians 4:3-6
Mark 9:2-9

Reflection on Sunday
Daily: Psalm 110:1-4

Monday
Exodus 19:7-25
Hebrews 2:1-4

Tuesday
Job 19:23-27
1 Timothy 3:14-16

Ash Wednesday
Joel 2:1-2, 12-17
Psalm 51:1-17
2 Corinthians 5:20b—6:10
Matthew 6:1-6, 16-21

The General Rule of Discipleship
To witness to Jesus Christ in the world and to follow his teachings
through acts of compassion, justice, worship, and devotion under the guidance of the Holy Spirit.

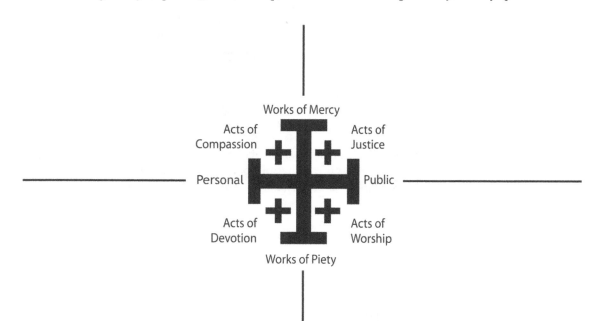

Word from John Wesley

. . . the true members of the Church of Christ "endeavour," with all possible diligence, with all care and pains, with unwearied patience, (and all will be little enough,) to "keep the unity of the Spirit in the bond of peace;" to preserve inviolate the same spirit of lowliness and meekness, of longsuffering, mutual forbearance, and love; and all these cemented and knit together by that sacred tie,—the peace of God filling the heart. Thus only can we be and continue living members of that Church which is the body of Christ.

Sermon 74: "Of the Church," § II.27

A Hymn from Charles Wesley

The meek and lowly heart,
That in our Saviour was,
To us his Spirit does impart,
And signs us with his cross:
Our nature's turned, our mind
Transformed in all its powers;
And both the witnesses are joined,
The Spirit of God with ours.

Whate'er our pardoning Lord
Commands, we gladly do,
And guided by his sacred Word
We all his steps pursue.
His glory our design,
We live our God to please;
And rise, with filial fear divine,
To perfect holiness.

(*Collection—1781*, #93:5 & 6)

Prayers, Comments & Questions

Holy God, you have revealed the glory of your love in Jesus Christ and have given us a share in your Spirit. May we who listen to Christ follow faithfully and, in the dark places where you send us, reveal the light of your gospel. Amen.

Lent

Forming Disciples Who Live as Jesus Lived

The primary purpose of Lent, from its beginnings, has been to provide a period of intense formation for those preparing to take on the covenant of baptism with the baptized, with baptism celebrated at Easter. Over time, as the early church's extensive three-year system of formation (called the catechumenate) fell into disuse, Lent became in practice primarily a time for penitence and increased acts of self-discipline, as well as, in some ways, particularly among Protestants, a kind of "extended Holy Week" for contemplating the suffering of Jesus.

With the renewal of the Christian Year brought about for Roman Catholics in Vatican II (early 1960s) and for Protestants coinciding with the development of the Revised Common Lectionary (1992), more and more Western Christians have recovered the idea, if not entirely the practices, of Lent as a season of preparation for baptism, reconciliation for the estranged, and final preparation for confirmation or reaffirmation by those baptized who are deemed ready to take the vows of baptism for themselves for the first time or in a deeper way.

Consequently, the readings you will experience on Sundays and weekdays during Lent are much more about how Jesus teaches his disciples to follow him and not about the sufferings of Jesus or his execution per se. And every year the Sunday readings correspond with key elements of the baptismal vows. If your congregation is not already providing accountable small groups to read and explore the implications of these readings, Sunday and/or daily, for living as the baptized, let me encourage you to gather a few Christian friends and create your own. Consider meeting face to face at least once weekly.

When you gather, read one of the gospel readings aloud three times, *lectio continua* style, paying attention the first time to what catches your attention, the second to what the thing that caught your attention is calling you to do, and the third to how you will respond in obedience to do it. Then share what you have gleaned from your reading with others in your small group. Decide how you will help each other be obedient to what you each have heard during the coming week.

Rev. Taylor Burton-Edwards

First Sunday in Lent

Preparation for Sunday
Daily: Psalm 25:1-10

Thursday
Daniel 9:1-14
1 John 1:3-10

Friday
Daniel 9:15-25a
2 Timothy 4:1-5

Saturday
Psalm 32
Matthew 9:2-13

Sunday
Genesis 9:8-17
Psalm 25:1-10
1 Peter 3:18-22
Mark 1:9-15

Reflection on Sunday
Daily: Psalm 77

Monday
Job 4:1-21
Ephesians 2:1-10

Tuesday
Job 5:8-27
1 Peter 3:8-18a

Wednesday
Proverbs 30:1-9
Matthew 4:1-11

The General Rule of Discipleship
To witness to Jesus Christ in the world and to follow his teachings
through acts of compassion, justice, worship, and devotion under the guidance of the Holy Spirit.

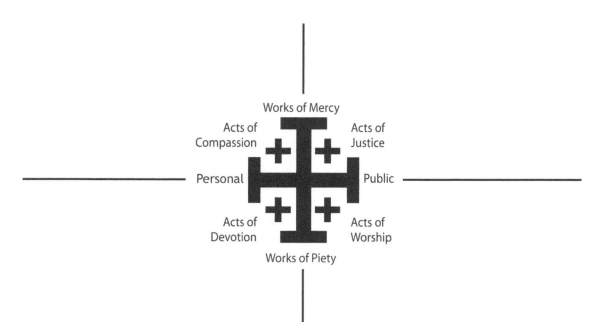

A Word from John Wesley

It is evil in itself. To separate ourselves from a body of living Christian, with whom we were before united, is a grievous breach of the law of love. It is the nature of love to unite us together; and the greater the love, the stricter the union. And while this continues in its strength, nothing can divide those whom love has united. It is only when our love grows could, that we can think of separating from our brethren. And this is certainly the case with any who willingly separate from their Christian brethren. The pretences for separation may be innumerable, but want of love is always the real cause; otherwise they would still hold the unity of the Spirit in the bound of peace.

Sermon 75: "On Schism," §I.11

A Hymn from Charles Wesley

Fain would I know as known by thee,
And feel the indigence I see;
Fain would I all my vileness own,
And deep beneath the burden groan;
Abhor the pride that lurks within,
Detest and loathe myself and sin.

Ah, give me, Lord, myself to feel,
My total misery reveal;
Ah, give me, Lord (I still would say),
A heart to mourn, a heart to pray;
My business this, my only care,
My life, my every breath be prayer!

(*Collection—1781*, #96:4 & 5)

Prayers, Comments & Questions

God of our salvation, your bow in the clouds proclaims your covenant with every living creature. Teach us your paths and lead us in your truth, that by your Holy Spirit, we may remember our baptismal vows and be keepers of your trust with earth and its inhabitants. Amen.

Second Sunday in Lent

Preparation for Sunday
Daily: Psalm 22:23-31

Thursday
Genesis 15:1-6, 12-18
Romans 3:21-31

Friday
Genesis 16:1-6
Romans 4:1-12

Saturday
Genesis 16:7-15
Mark 8:27-30

Sunday
Genesis 17:1-7, 15-16
Psalm 22:23-31
Romans 4:13-25
Mark 8:31-38

Reflection on Sunday
Daily: Psalm 105:1-11, 37-45

Monday
Genesis 21:1-7
Hebrews 1:8-12

Tuesday
Genesis 22:1-19
Hebrews 11:1-3, 13-19

Wednesday
Jeremiah 30:12-22
John 12:36-43

The General Rule of Discipleship
To witness to Jesus Christ in the world and to follow his teachings
through acts of compassion, justice, worship, and devotion under the guidance of the Holy Spirit.

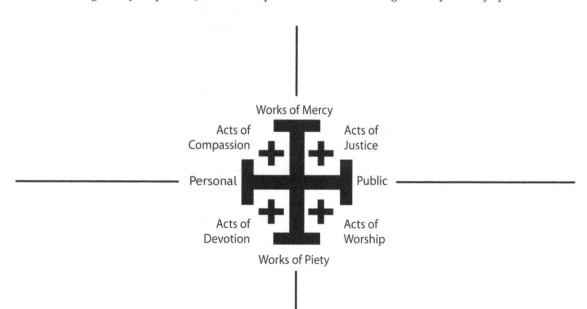

A Word from John Wesley

What is then the perfection of which man is capable while he dwells in a corruptible body It is the complying with that kind command, "My son, give me thy heart." It is the "loving the Lord his God with all his heart, and with all his soul, and with all his mind." This is the sum of Christian perfection: It is all comprised in that one word, Love. The first branch of it is the love of God: And as he that loves God loves his brother also, it is inseparably connected with the second: "Thou shalt love thy neighbour as thyself:" Thou shalt love every man as thy own soul, as Christ loved us. "On these two commandments hang all the law and the prophets:" These contain the whole of Christian perfection.

Sermon 76: § I.4

A Hymn from Charles Wesley

Jesu, my heart's desire obtain!
My earnest suit present and gain,
My fullness of corruption show,
The knowledge of myself bestow;
A deeper displicence at sin,
A sharper sense of hell within,
A stronger struggling to get free,
A keener appetite for thee!

O sovereign Love, to thee I cry!
Give me thyself, or else I die!
Save me from death, from hell set free—
Death, hell, are but the want of thee.
Quickened by thy imparted flame,
Saved, when possessed of thee, I am;
My life, my only heaven thou art!
O might I feel thee in my heart!

(*Collection—1781*, #97:3 & 4)

Prayers, Comments & Questions

God of Sarah and Abraham, long ago you embraced your people in covenant and promised them your blessing. Strengthen us in faith, that, with your disciples of every age, we may proclaim your deliverance in Jesus Christ to generations yet unborn. Amen.

Third Sunday in Lent

Preparation for Sunday
Daily: Psalm 19

Thursday
Exodus 19:1-9a
1 Peter 2:4-10

Friday
Exodus 19:9b-15
Acts 7:30-40

Saturday
Exodus 19:16-25
Mark 9:2-8

Sunday
Exodus 20:1-17
Psalm 19
1 Corinthians 1:18-25
John 2:13-22

Reflection on Sunday
Daily: Psalm 84

Monday
1 Kings 6:1-4, 21-22
1 Corinthians 3:10-23

Tuesday
2 Chronicles 29:1-11, 16-19
Hebrews 9:23-28

Wednesday
Ezra 6:1-16
Mark 11:15-19

The General Rule of Discipleship
To witness to Jesus Christ in the world and to follow his teachings
through acts of compassion, justice, worship, and devotion under the guidance of the Holy Spirit.

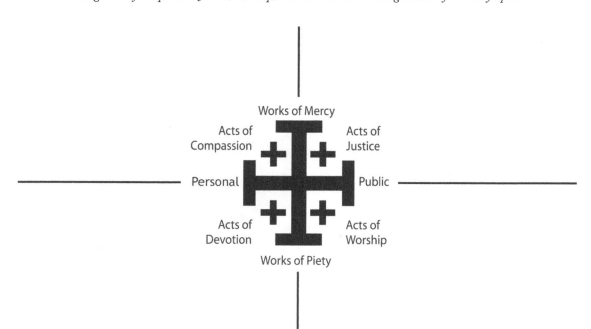

Works of Mercy

Acts of Compassion

Acts of Justice

Personal

Public

Acts of Devotion

Acts of Worship

Works of Piety

A Word from John Wesley

The true God is also the Redeemer of all the children of men. It pleased the Father to lay upon him the iniquities of us all, that by the one oblation of himself once offered, when he tasted death for every man, he might make a full and sufficient sacrifice, oblation, and satisfaction for the sins of the whole world.

Sermon 77: "Spiritual Worship," § I.7

A Hymn from Charles Wesley

Saviour, Prince of Israel's race,
See me from thy lofty throne,
Give the sweet relenting grace,
Soften this obdurate stone!
Stone to flesh, O God, convert,
Cast a look and break my heart!

By thy Spirit, Lord, reprove,
All mine inmost sins reveal;
Sins against thy light and love
Let me see, and let me feel,
Sins that crucified my God,
Spilt again thy precious blood.

(*Collection—1781*, #98:1 & 2)

Prayers, Comments & Questions

Holy One, creator of the stars and seas, your steadfast love is shown to every living thing: your word calls forth countless worlds and souls; your law revives and refreshes. Forgive our misuse of your gifts, that we may be transformed by your wisdom to manifest for others the mercy of our crucified and risen Lord. Amen.

Fourth Sunday in Lent

Preparation for Sunday
Daily: Psalm 107:1-3, 17-22

Thursday
Genesis 9:8-17
Ephesians 1:3-6

Friday
Daniel 12:5-13
Ephesians 1:7-14

Saturday
Numbers 20:22-29
John 3:1-13

Sunday
Numbers 21:4-9
Psalm 107:1-3, 17-22
Ephesians 2:1-10
John 3:14-21

Reflection on Sunday
Daily: Psalm 107:1-16

Monday
Exodus 15:22-27
Hebrews 3:1-6

Tuesday
Numbers 20:1-13
1 Corinthians 10:6-13

Wednesday
Isaiah 60:15-22
John 8:12-20

The General Rule of Discipleship
To witness to Jesus Christ in the world and to follow his teachings
through acts of compassion, justice, worship, and devotion under the guidance of the Holy Spirit.

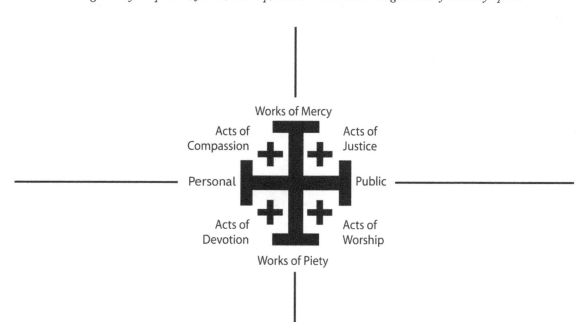

A Word from John Wesley

God created all things for himself; more especially all intelligent spirits. (And indeed it seems that intelligence, in some kind or degree, is inseparable from spiritual beings; that intelligence is as essential to spirits as extension is to matter.) He made those more directly for himself, to know, love, and enjoy him. As the sun is the centre of the solar system, so (as far as we may compare material things with spiritual) we need not scruple to affirm that God is the centre of spirits. And as long as they are united to Him, created spirits are at rest: They are at rest so long, and no longer, as they "attend upon the Lord without distraction."

Sermon 79: "On Dissipation," ¶ 4

A Hymn from Charles Wesley

O that I could repent!
With all my idols part,
And to thy gracious eye present
An humble, contrite heart!
An heart with grief oppressed
For having grieved my God;
A troubled heart, that cannot rest
Till sprinkled with thy blood!

Jesus, on me bestow
The penitent desire;
With true sincerity of woe
My aching breast inspire;
With softening pity look,
And melt my hardness down;
Strike, with thy lovers resistless stroke,
And break this heart of stone!

(*Collection—1781*, #99)

Prayers, Comments & Questions

Steadfast God, you reached out to us in mercy even when we rebel against your holy call and prefer to walk in disobedience rather than in the way of your divine truth. Soften our hearts with the warmth of your love, that we may know your Son alive within us, redeeming us and raising us up into your eternal presence. Amen.

Fifth Sunday in Lent

Preparation for Sunday
Daily: Psalm 51:1-12

Thursday
Isaiah 30:15-18
Hebrews 4:1-13

Friday
Exodus 30:1-10
Hebrews 4:14—5:4

Saturday
Habakkuk 3:2-13
John 12:1-11

Sunday
Jeremiah 31:31-34
Psalm 51:1-12
Hebrews 5:5-10
John 12:20-33

Reflection on Sunday
Daily: Psalm 119:9-16

Monday
Isaiah 43:8-13
2 Corinthians 3:4-11

Tuesday
Isaiah 44:1-8
Acts 2:14-24

Wednesday
Haggai 2:1-9, 20-23
John 12:34-50

The General Rule of Discipleship
*To witness to Jesus Christ in the world and to follow his teachings
through acts of compassion, justice, worship, and devotion under the guidance of the Holy Spirit.*

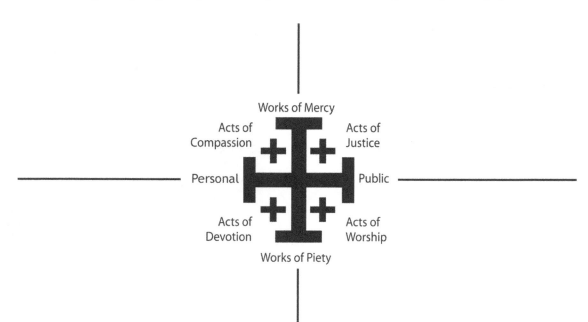

Works of Mercy

Acts of Compassion

Acts of Justice

Personal

Public

Acts of Devotion

Acts of Worship

Works of Piety

A Word from John Wesley

But for what reasons is the friendship of the world so absolutely prohibited Why are we so strictly required to abstain from it? For two general reasons: First, because it is a sin in itself: Secondly, because it is attended with most dreadful consequences. First, it is a sin in itself; and indeed, a sin of no common dye. According to the oracles of God, friendship with the world is no less than spiritual adultery. All who are guilty of it are addressed by the Holy Ghost in those terms: "Ye adulterers and adulteresses." It is plainly violating of our marriage contract with God, by loving the creature more than the Creator; in flat contradiction to that kind command, "My son, give me thine heart."

Sermon 80: "On Friendship With The World," ¶ 13

A Hymn from Charles Wesley

O that I could revere
My much offended God!
O that I could but stand in fear
Of thy afflicting rod!
If mercy cannot draw,
Thou, by thy threat'nings, move,
And keep an abject soul in awe
That will not yield to love.

Thou great, tremendous God,
The conscious awe impart;
The grace be now on me bestowed,
The tender, fleshly heart;
For Jesu's sake alone
The stony heart remove,
And melt at last, O melt me down
Into the mould of love.

(*Collection—1781*, #100:1 & 3)

Prayers, Comments & Questions

God of suffering and glory, in Jesus Christ you reveal the way of life through the path of obedience. Inscribe your law in our hearts, that in life we may not stray from you, but may be your people. Amen.

Sixth Sunday in Lent
Passion/Palm Sunday

Preparation for Sunday
Daily: Psalm 118:1-2, 19-29

Thursday
Deuteronomy 16:1-8
Philippians 2:1-11

Friday
Jeremiah 33:1-9
Philippians 2:12-18

Saturday
Jeremiah 33:10-16
Mark 10:32-34, 46-52

Sunday
Liturgy of the Palms
Mark 11:1-11 or
John 12:12-16

Liturgy of the Passion
Isaiah 50:4-9a
Psalm 31:9-16
Philippians 2:5-11
Mark 14:1—15:47

The General Rule of Discipleship
To witness to Jesus Christ in the world and to follow his teachings
through acts of compassion, justice, worship, and devotion under the guidance of the Holy Spirit.

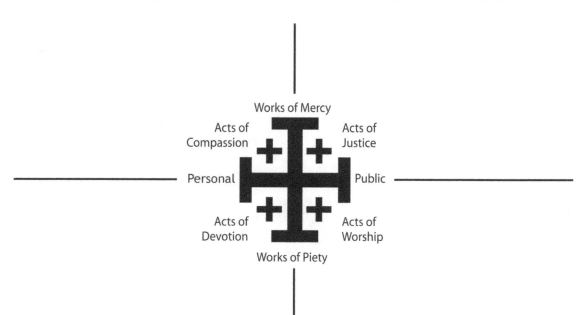

A Word from John Wesley

A Fifth and more weighty reason for fasting is, that it is an help to prayer; particularly when we set apart larger portions of time for private prayer. Then especially it is that God is often pleased to lift up the souls of his servants above all the things of earth, and sometimes to rap them up, as it were, into the third heavens. And it is chiefly, as it is an help to prayer, that it has so frequently been found a means, in the hand of God, of confirming and increasing, not one virtue, not chastity only, (as some have idly imagined, without any ground either from Scripture, reason, or experience,) but also seriousness of spirit, earnestness, sensibility and tenderness of conscience, deadness to the world, and consequently the love of God, and every holy and heavenly affection.

Sermon 27: "Upon Our Lord's Sermon on the Mount VII," § II.6

A Hymn from Charles Wesley

All that pass by, To Jesus draw near,
He utters a cry, Ye sinners, give ear!
From hell to retrieve you
He spreads out his hands;
Now, now to receive you,
He graciously stands.

If any man thirst, And happy would be,
The vilest and worst May come unto me,
May drink of my Spirit,
Excepted is none,
Lay claim to my merit,
And take for his own.

Whoever receives
The life-giving word,
In Jesus believes,
His God and his Lord,
In him a pure river
Of life shall arise,
Shall in the believer
Spring up to the skies.

(*Collection*—1781, #3:1-3)

Prayers, Comments & Questions

Sovereign God, you have established your rule over the human heart, not by force but by the servant example of Jesus Christ. Move us by your Spirit to join us in your Spirit to join the joyful procession of those who confess Christ Jesus with their tongues and praise him with their lives. Amen.

Holy Week

The Cost of Discipleship and Salvation

Lent moves into Holy Week beginning with Passion/Palm Sunday. This is the time we remember the final week of Jesus in Jerusalem, his last actions with his disciples, his arrest, his trial, his torture, and his execution. The daily readings (Monday through Saturday) are the same all three years, established by long tradition. And these are readings intended to be read and reflected upon in gathered community. Many congregations will have planned gatherings for worship on Maundy Thursday and Good Friday. Fewer may be likely to gather for the solemn vigil of Holy Saturday morning or the other weekdays.

The formational power of this week is greatly enhanced if you do gather every day in some way. Perhaps you may find a time each evening to meet in homes, or a "third place," or perhaps you may decide to gather "virtually" through an online venue such as Skype, Facebook, or Twitter. While during Lent the focus of the readings was to commit to what you might do, during Holy Week the purpose is simply to let them sink in and allow the readings to work their work in your gathered community. Read the scriptures. Pray for the church and the world. Bid each other the peace of Christ. And continue to watch and pray for what the Spirit will put to death and bring to new life in each of you.

Rev. Taylor Burton-Edwards

Monday

Isaiah 42:1-9
Psalm 36:5-11
Hebrews 9:11-15
John 12:1-11

Collect for Monday of Holy Week

God of steadfast love, light of the blind and liberator of the oppressed, we see your holy purpose in the tender compassion of Jesus, who calls us into new and living friendship with you. May we, who take shelter in the shadow of your wings, be filled with the grace of his tender caring; may we, who stumble in selfish darkness, see your glory in the light of his self-giving. We ask this through him whose suffering is victorious, Jesus Christ our Savior. Amen.

Tuesday

Isaiah 49:1-7
Psalm 71:1-14
1 Corinthians 1:18-31
John 12:20-36

Collect for Tuesday of Holy Week

Holy and immortal God, from earliest times you have named us and called us into discipleship. Teach us to follow the One whose light scatters the darkness of our world, that we may walk as children of the light. Amen.

Wednesday

Isaiah 50:4-9a
Psalm 70
Hebrews 12:1-3
John 13:21-32

Collect for Wednesday of Holy Week

Troubled God, in every generation you call your people to contend against the brutality of sin and betrayal. Keep us steadfast even in our fear and uncertainty, that we may follow where Jesus has led the way. Amen.

The Three Days

Holy Thursday

Exodus 12:1-14
Psalm 116:1-2, 12-19
1 Corinthians 11:23-26
John 13:1-17, 31b-35

Collect for Holy Thursday

Eternal God, in the sharing of a meal your Son established a new covenant for all people, and in the washing of feet he showed us the dignity of service. Grant that by the power of your Holy Spirit these signs of our life in faith may speak again to our hearts, feed our spirits, and refresh our bodies. Amen.

Good Friday

Isaiah 52:13—53:12
Psalm 22
Hebrews 10:16-25
John 18:1—19:42

Collect for Good Friday

Grieving God, on the cross your Son embraced death even as he had embraced life: faithfully and with good courage. Grant that we who have been born out of his wounded side may hold fast to our faith in him exalted and may find mercy in all times of need. Amen.

Holy Saturday

Job 14:1-14
Psalm 31:1-4, 15-16
1 Peter 4:1-8
John 19:38-42

Collect for Holy Saturday

Eternal God, rock and refuge: with roots grown old in the earth, river beds run dry, and flowers withered in the field, we wait for revival and release. Abide with us until we come alive in the sunrise of your glory. Amen.

Hymn for Holy Week

O Love divine, what has thou done!
The immortal God hath died for me!
The Father's coeternal Son
bore all my sins upon the tree.
The immortal God hath died for me!
My Lord, my Love, is crucified!

Is crucified for me and you,
to bring us rebels back to God.
Believe, believe the record true,
ye all are bought with Jesus' blood.
Pardon for all flows from his side:
My Lord, my Love, is crucified!

Behold him, all ye that pass by,
the bleeding Prince of life and peace!
Come, sinners, see your Savior die,
and say, "Was ever grief like his?"
Come, feel with me his blood applied:
My Lord, my Love, is crucified!

(*Collection*—1781, #27, 88.88.88)

Easter Season

Teaching and Preparing to Unleash Salvation

The first service of Easter is full of readings! This is the Great Vigil of Easter, offered after sundown on Saturday night. It is a powerful service of Fire, Word, Water, and Table. We light the new fire, signifying the light of Christ overcoming the world. We rehearse the story of God's salvation, from creation and exodus to the resurrection of Christ. We exult in Alleluias. We baptize those who have been preparing during Lent and vigiling in prayer with us during Holy Week. And we celebrate the feast of our redemption around the Lord's Table. If your congregation does not yet celebrate this amazing and ancient Christian service, find one that does (most Episcopal, Roman Catholic, and many Lutheran congregations will!) and take folks with you, including your pastor, so they may see, hear, smell, taste, and touch, and perhaps develop plans to bring others or create one for your congregation next year.

Easter, the Season of the Passover of our Lord, begins with a bang! And it concludes with another one, fifty days later at Pentecost, when we celebrate the coming of the Holy Spirit on the early Christians long ago, and all the ways the Spirit is moving among us here and now.

Between these days of celebration are weeks of further formation so that your celebration, come Pentecost, may be full indeed. Easter Season is a time especially for helping the newly baptized with all the baptized grow in their understanding of Christian doctrine and to identify their gifts and callings for ministry in Christ's name. On Easter, both at the Great Vigil and again on Sunday morning, we exult in the resurrection of Jesus Christ from the dead. On Pentecost, we exult in what the Spirit is doing in the lives of those reborn or recommitted, and we bless and commission them for their ministries among us. And in the weeks between, in Sunday and in daily readings, we prepare ourselves to grow in our knowledge and love of God, and to sharpen our own passions and skills for ministry in Christ's name and the Spirit's power.

Rev. Taylor Burton-Edwards

Resurrection of the Lord

Sunday
Acts 10:34-43
Psalm 118:1-2, 14-24
1 Corinthians 15:1-11
John 20:1-18
or
Mark 16:1-8

Easter Evening
Isaiah 25:6-9
Psalm 114
1 Corinthians 5:6b-8
Luke 24:13-49

Reflecting on Sunday
Daily: Psalm 118:1-2, 14-24

Monday
Genesis 1:1-19
1 Corinthians 15:35-49

Tuesday
Genesis 1:20—2:4a
1 Corinthians 15:50-58

Wednesday
Song of Solomon 3:1-11
Mark 16:1-8

The General Rule of Discipleship
To witness to Jesus Christ in the world and to follow his teachings
through acts of compassion, justice, worship, and devotion under the guidance of the Holy Spirit.

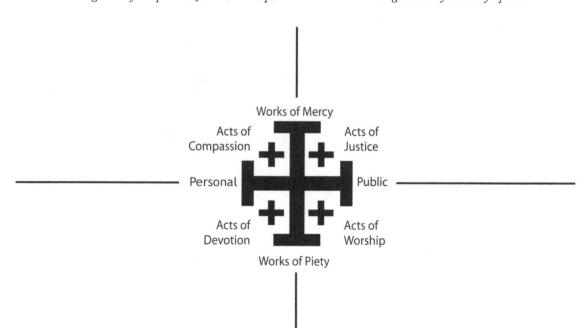

A Word from John Wesley

The necessary fruit of this love of God is the love of our neighbour; of every soul which God hath made; not excepting our enemies; not excepting those who are now "despitefully using and persecuting us;"—a love whereby we love every man as ourselves; as we love our own souls. Nay, our Lord has expressed it still more strongly, teaching us to "love one another even as He hath loved us." Accordingly, the commandment written in the hearts of all those that love God, is no other than this, "As I have loved you, so love ye one another."

Sermon 18: "The Marks of the New Birth," § III.3

A Hymn from Charles Wesley

Sinners, dismiss your fear,
The joyful tidings hear!
This the word that Jesus said,
O believe, and feel it true,
Christ is risen from the dead,
Lives the Lord who died for you!

Why the art thou cast down,
Thou poor afflicted one?
Full of doubts, and griefs, and fears,
Look into that open grave!
Died He not to dry thy tears?
Rose He not thy soul to save?

To purge thy guilty stain
He died, and rose again:
Wherefore does thou weep and mourn?
Sinner, lift thine heart and eye,
Turn thee, to thy Jesus turn,
See thy loving Savior nigh.

(*Hymns for our Lord's Resurrection*—1746, #2:1, 3 & 5)

Prayers, Comments & Questions

Creator of the universe, you made the world in beauty, and you restore all things in glory through the victory of Jesus Christ. We pray that wherever your image is still disfigured by poverty, sickness, selfishness, war, and greed, the new creation in Jesus Christ may appear in justice, love, and peace, to the glory of your name. Amen.

Second Sunday of Easter

Preparation for Sunday
Daily: Psalm 133

Thursday
Daniel 1:1-21
Acts 2:42-47

Friday
Daniel 2:1-23
Acts 4:23-31

Saturday
Daniel 2:24-49
John 12:44-50

Sunday
Acts 4:32-35
Psalm 133
1 John 1:1—2:2
John 20:19-31

Reflection on Sunday
Daily: Psalm 135

Monday
Daniel 3:1-30
1 John 2:3-11

Tuesday
Daniel 6:1-28
1 John 2:12-17

Wednesday
Isaiah 26:1-15
Mark 12:18-27

The General Rule of Discipleship
To witness to Jesus Christ in the world and to follow his teachings
through acts of compassion, justice, worship, and devotion under the guidance of the Holy Spirit.

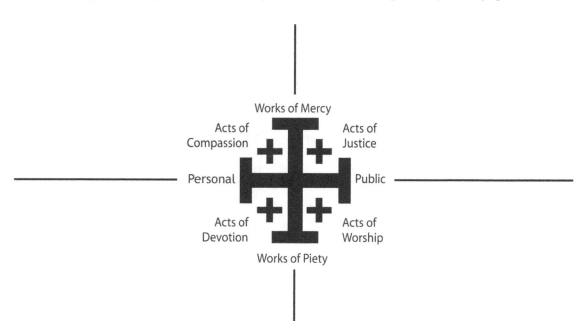

A Word from John Wesley

Let him that most assuredly standeth, take heed lest he fall" into murmuring; lest he say in his hear, "Surely no one's case is like mine; no one was ever tried like me." Yea, ten thousand. "There was no temptation taken you," but such as is "common to man;" such as you might reasonably expect, if you considered what you are; a sinner born to die; a sinful inhabitant of a mortal body, liable to numberless inward and outward sufferings;—and where you are; in a shattered, disordered world. surrounded by evil men, and evil spirits. Consider this, and you will not repine at the common lot, the general condition of humanity.

Sermon 82: "On Temptation," § III.7

A Hymn from Charles Wesley

All ye that seek the Lord who died,
Your God for sinners crucified,
Prevent the earliest dawn, and come
To worship at his sacred tomb.

Bring the sweet spices of your sighs,
Your contrite hearts, and streaming eyes,
Your sad complaints, and humble fears;
Come, and embalm him with your tears.

While thus ye love your souls t'employ,
Your sorrow shall be turned to joy:
Now, now let all your grief be oe'er
Believe, and ye shall weep no more.

Haste then, ye souls that first believe,
Who dare the Gospel-word receive,
Your faith with joyful hearts confess,
Be bold, be Jesus' witnesses.

Go tell the followers of your Lord
Their Jesus is to life restored;
He lives, that they his life may find;
He lives, to quicken all mankind.

(*Hymns for our Lord's Resurrection*—1746, #1:1-3, 11 & 12)

Prayers, Comments & Questions

Light of the world, shine upon us and disperse the clouds of our selfishness, that we may reflect the power of the Resurrection in our life together. Amen.

Third Sunday of Easter

Preparation for Sunday
Daily: Psalm 4

Thursday
Daniel 9:1-19
1 John 2:18-25

Friday
Daniel 10:2-19
1 John 2:26-28

Saturday
Acts 3:1-10
Luke 22:24-30

Sunday
Acts 3:12-19
Psalm 4
1 John 3:1-7
Luke 24:36b-48

Reflection on Sunday
Daily: Psalm 150

Monday
Jeremiah 30:1-11a
1 John 3:10-16

Tuesday
Hosea 5:15—6:6
2 John 1-6

Wednesday
Proverbs 9:1-6
Mark 16:9-18

The General Rule of Discipleship
*To witness to Jesus Christ in the world and to follow his teachings
through acts of compassion, justice, worship, and devotion under the guidance of the Holy Spirit.*

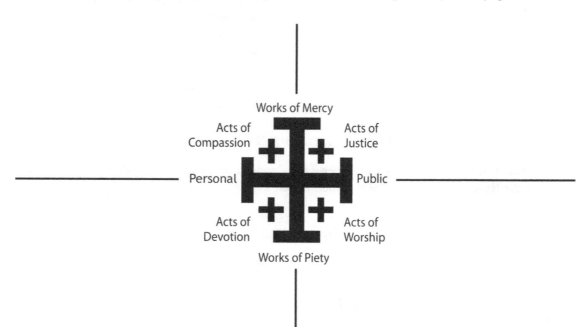

A Word from John Wesley

But what may we understand by the work of patience "Let patience have its perfect work." It seems to mean, let it have its full fruit or effect. And what is the fruit which the Spirit of God is accustomed to produce hereby, in the heart of a believer One immediate fruit of patience is peace: A sweet tranquility of mind; a serenity of spirit, which can never be found, unless where patience reigns. And this peace often rises into joy. Even in the midst of various temptations, those that are enabled "in patience to possess their souls," can witness, not only quietness of spirit, but triumph and exultation. This both

Lays the rough paths of peevish nature even, And opens in each breast a little heaven.

Sermon 83: "On Patience," ¶ 5

A Hymn from Charles Wesley

Who can now presume to fear?
Who despair his Lord to see?
Show thyself alive to me?
Yes, my God, I dare not doubt,
Thou shalt all my sins remove;
Thou hast cast a legion out,
Thou wilt perfect me in Love.

Surely thou hast called me now!
Now I hear the voice divine,
At thy wounded feet I bow,
Wounded for whose sins but mine!
I have nailed him to the tree,
I have sent him to the grave:
But the Lord is risen for me,
Hold of him by faith I have.

Hear, ye brethren of the Lord,
(Such he you vouchsafes to call)
O believe the Gospel-Word,
Christ hath died, and rose for all:
Turn ye from your sins to God,
Haste to Galilee, and see
Him, who bought thee with his blood,
Him, who rose to live in thee.

(*Hymns for Our Lord's Resurrection*—1746, #3:4, 5 & 7)

Prayers, Comments & Questions

Holy and righteous God, you raised Christ from the dead and glorified him at your right hand. Let the words of scripture fulfilled in Jesus your Son burn within our hearts and open our minds to recognize him in the breaking of bread. Amen.

Fourth Sunday of Easter

Preparation for Sunday
Daily: Psalm 23

Thursday
Genesis 30:25-43
Acts 3:17-26

Friday
Genesis 46:28—47:6
Acts 4:1-4

Saturday
Genesis 48:8-19
Mark 6:30-34

Sunday
Acts 4:5-12
Psalm 23
1 John 3:16-24
John 10:11-18

Reflection on Sunday
Daily: Psalm 95

Monday
1 Samuel 16:1-13
1 Peter 5:1-5

Tuesday
1 Chronicles 11:1-9
Revelation 7:13-17

Wednesday
Micah 7:8-20
Mark 14:26-31

The General Rule of Discipleship
To witness to Jesus Christ in the world and to follow his teachings
through acts of compassion, justice, worship, and devotion under the guidance of the Holy Spirit.

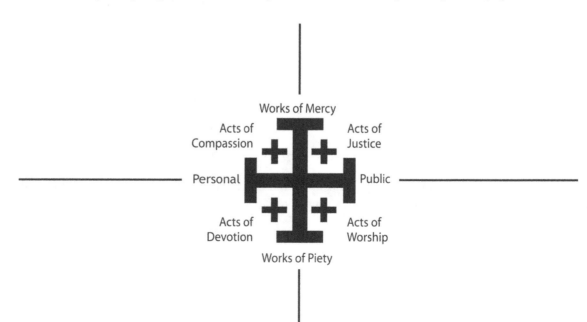

A Word from John Wesley

What is religion then It is easy to answer, if we consult the oracles of God. According to these it lies in one single point; it is neither more nor less than love; it is love which "is the fulfilling of the law, the end of the commandment." Religion is the love of God and our neighbour; that is, every man under heaven. This love ruling the whole life, animating all our tempers and passions, directing all our thoughts, words, and actions, is "pure religion and undefiled."

Sermon 84: "The Important Question," § III.2

A Hymn from Charles Wesley

Jesus, the Rising Lord of all,
His Love to man commends,
Poor worms he blushes not to call
His brethren and his friends.

Who basely all forsook their Lord
In his distress, and fled,
To these he sends the joyful Word,
When risen from the dead.

Sinners, I rose again to show
Your sins are all forgiven,
And mount above the skies, that you
May follow me to Heaven.

(*Hymns for Our Lord's Resurrection—1746–1781*, 4:1, 2 & 6)

Prayers, Comments & Questions

Shepherd of all, by laying down your life for your flock you reveal your love for all. Lead us from the place of death to the place of abundant life, that guided by your care for us, we may rightly offer our lives in love for you and our neighbors. Amen.

Fifth Sunday of Easter

Preparation for Sunday
Daily: Psalm 22:25-31

Thursday
Amos 8:1-7
Acts 8:1b-8

Friday
Amos 8:11-13
Acts 8:9-25

Saturday
Amos 9:7-15
Mark 4:30-32

Sunday
Acts 8:26-40
Psalm 22:25-31
1 John 4:7-21
John 15:1-8

Reflection on Sunday
Daily: Psalm 80

Monday
Isaiah 5:1-7
Galatians 5:16-26

Tuesday
Isaiah 32:9-20
James 3:17-18

Wednesday
Isaiah 65:17-25
John 14:18-31

The General Rule of Discipleship
*To witness to Jesus Christ in the world and to follow his teachings
through acts of compassion, justice, worship, and devotion under the guidance of the Holy Spirit.*

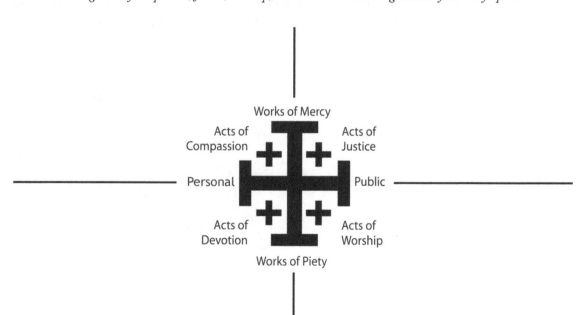

A Word from John Wesley

But what are the steps which the Scripture directs us to take, in the working out of our own salvation The Prophet Isaiah gives us a general answer, touching the first steps which we are to take: "Cease to do evil; learn to do well." If ever you desire that God should work in you that faith whereof cometh both present and eternal salvation, by the grace already given, fly from all sin as from the face of a serpent; carefully avoid every evil word and work; yea, abstain from all appearance of evil. And "learn to do well."

Sermon 85: "On Working Out Our Own Salvation," § II.4

A Hymn from Charles Wesley

Object of all our knowledge here,
Our one desire, and hope below,
Jesus, the Crucified, draw near,
And with thy disciples go:
Our thoughts and words to thee are known,
We commune of thyself alone.

How can it be, our reason cries,
That God should leave his throne above?
Is it for man the Immortal dies!
For man, who tramples on his Love!
For Man, who nailed him to the tree!
O Love! O God! He dies for me!

Ah! Lord, if thou indeed art ours,
If thou for us hast burst the tomb,
Visit us with thy quickening powers,
Come to thy mournful followers come,
Thyself to thy weak members join,
And fill us with the Life Divine.

(*Hymns for our Lord's Resurrection*—1746, #5:1, 2 & 5)

Prayers, Comments & Questions

God, you sent your Son into the world that we might live through him. May we abide in his risen love so that we may bear the fruit of love for one another and know the fullness of joy. Amen.

Sixth Sunday of Easter

Preparation for Sunday
Daily: Psalm 98

Thursday
Isaiah 49:5-6
Acts 10:1-34

Friday
Isaiah 42:5-9
Acts 10:34-43

Saturday
Deuteronomy 32:44-47
Mark 10:42-45

Sunday
Acts 10:44-48
Psalm 98
1 John 5:1-6
John 15:9-17

Reflection on Sunday
Daily: Psalm 93

Monday
Deuteronomy 7:1-11
1 Timothy 6:11-12

Tuesday
Deuteronomy 11:1-17
1 Timothy 6:13-16

Wednesday
Deuteronomy 11:18-21
Mark 16:19-20

The General Rule of Discipleship
To witness to Jesus Christ in the world and to follow his teachings
through acts of compassion, justice, worship, and devotion under the guidance of the Holy Spirit.

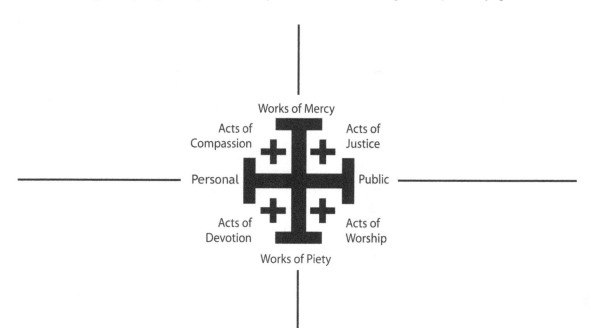

A Word from John Wesley

Be zealous of good works, of works of piety, as well as works of mercy; family prayer, and crying to God in secret. Fast in secret, and "your Father which seeth in secret, he will reward you openly." "Search the Scriptures:" Hear them in public, read them in private, and meditate therein. At every opportunity, be a partaker of the Lord's Supper. "Do this in remembrance of him: and he will meet you at his own table. Let your conversation be with the children of God; and see that it "be in grace, seasoned with salt." As ye have time, do good unto all men; to their souls and to their bodies. And herein "be ye steadfast, unmovable, always abounding in the work of the Lord.""

Sermon 85: "On Working Out Our Own Salvation," § II.4

A Hymn from Charles Wesley

Come in, with thy disciples sit,
Nor suffer us to ask in vain,
Nourish us, Lord, with living meat.
Our souls with heavenly bread sustain;
Break to us now the mystic bread,
And bid us on thy body feed.

Honor the means ordained by thee,
The great unbloody sacrifice,
The deep tremendous mystery;
Thyself in our inlightened eyes
Now in the broken bread make known,
And shew us thou art all our own.

(*Hymns for our Lord's Resurrection*—1746, #6:5 & 6)

Prayers, Comments & Questions

Faithful God, make our hearts bold with love for one another. Pour out your Spirit upon all people, that we may live your justice and sing in praise the new song of your marvelous victory. Amen.

Seventh Sunday of Easter

Preparation for Sunday
Daily: Psalm 47

Thursday,
Ascension of the Lord
Acts 1:1-11
Psalm 47 or Psalm 93
Ephesians 1:15-23
Luke 24:44-53

Friday
Exodus 24:15-18
Revelation 1:9-18

Saturday
Deuteronomy 34:1-7
John 16:4-11

Sunday
Acts 1:15-17, 21-26
Psalm 1
1 John 5:9-13
John 17:6-19

Reflection on Sunday
Daily: Psalm 115

Monday
Exodus 28:29-38
Philippians 1:3-11

Tuesday
Numbers 8:5-22
Titus 1:1-9

Wednesday
Ezra 9:5-15
John 16:16-24

The General Rule of Discipleship
To witness to Jesus Christ in the world and to follow his teachings
through acts of compassion, justice, worship, and devotion under the guidance of the Holy Spirit.

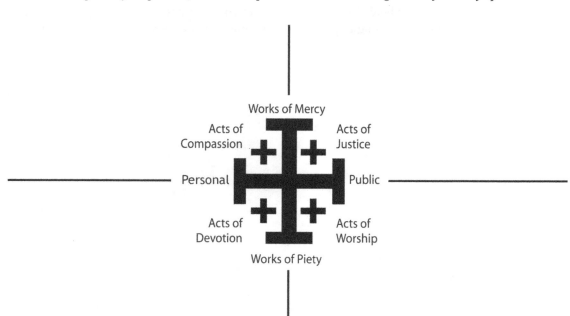

A Word from John Wesley

God worketh in you; therefore you can work: Otherwise it would be impossible. If he did not work it would be impossible for you to work out your own salvation. "With man this is impossible," saith our Lord, "for a rich man to enter into the kingdom of heaven." Yea, it is impossible for any man, for any that is born of a woman, unless God work in him. Seeing all men are by nature not only sick, but "dead in trespasses and sins," it is not possible for them to do anything well till God raises them from the dead. It was impossible for Lazarus to come forth, till the Lord had given him life. And it is equally impossible for us to come out of our sins, yea, or to make the least motion toward it, till He who hath all power in heaven and earth calls our dead souls into life.

Sermon 85: "On Working Out Our Own Salvation," § III.3

A Hymn from Charles Wesley

Rejoice, the Lord is King!
Your Lord and King adore,
Mortals, give thanks and sing,
And triumph evermore;
Lift up your heart, lift up your voice,
Rejoice, again, I say, Rejoice.

Jesus the Savior reigns,
The God of Truth and Love,
When he had purged our stains,
He took his seat above:
Lift up your heart, lift up your voice,
Rejoice, again, I say, rejoice.

(*Hymns for our Lord's Resurrection*—1746, #8:1 & 2)

Prayers, Comments & Questions

Gracious God, in the resurrection of your Son Jesus Christ, you have given us eternal life and glorified your name in all the world. Refresh our souls with the living streams of your truth, that in our unity, your joy may be complete. Amen.

Day of Pentecost

Preparation for Sunday
Daily: Psalm 33:12-22

Thursday
Genesis 2:4b-7
1 Corinthians 15:42b-49

Friday
Job 37:1-13
1 Corinthians 15:50-57

Saturday
Exodus 15:6-11
John 7:37-39

Sunday
Acts 2:1-21
Psalm 104:24-34, 35b
Romans 8:22-27
John 15:26-27; 16:4b-15

Reflection on Sunday
Daily: Psalm 104:24-34, 35b

Monday
Joel 2:18-29
1 Corinthians 12:4-11

Tuesday
Genesis 11:1-9
1 Corinthians 12:12-27

Wednesday
Ezekiel 37:1-14
John 20:19-23

The General Rule of Discipleship
To witness to Jesus Christ in the world and to follow his teachings
through acts of compassion, justice, worship, and devotion under the guidance of the Holy Spirit.

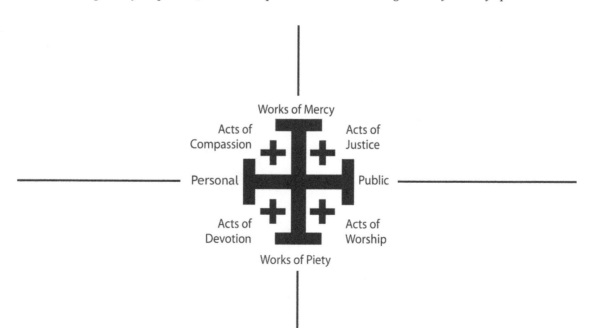

A Word from John Wesley

Therefore inasmuch as God works in you, you are now able to work out your own salvation. Since he worketh in you of his own good pleasure, without any merit of yours, both to will and to do, it is possible for you to fulfil all righteousness. It is possible for you to "love God, because he hath first loved us;" and to "walk in love," after the pattern of our great Master. We know, indeed, that word of his to be absolutely true: "Without me ye can do nothing." But on the other hand, we know, every believer can say "I can do all things through Christ that strengtheneth me."

Sermon 85: "On Working Out Our Own Salvation," § III.5

A Hymn from Charles Wesley

Father, if justly still we claim
To us and ours the promise made,
To us be graciously the same,
And crown with living fire our head.

Our claim admit, and from above
Of holiness the spirit shower;
Of wise discernment, humble love,
And zeal, and unity, and power.

The spirit of convincing speech,
Of power demonstrative impart,
Such as may every conscience reach,
And sound the unbelieving heart.

The spirit of refining fire,
Searching the inmost of the mind,
To purge all fierce and foul desire,
And kindle life more pure and kind.

(*Collection—1781*, #444:1-4)

Prayers, Comments & Questions

Creator Spirit and Giver of Life, make the dry, bleached bones of our lives live and breathe and grow again, as you did of old. Pour out your Spirit upon the whole creation. Come in rushing wind and flashing fire to turn the sin and sorrow within us into faith, power, and delight. Amen.

Season after Pentecost

Disciples in Ministry in Christ's Name and the Spirit's Power

This season is sometimes also referred to as "Ordinary Time," but it is intended to be far from "ordinary" in terms of its purposes in supporting and strengthening your discipleship to Jesus Christ. The word *Ordinary* here actually only refers to the "ordinal numbers" (first, second, third, and so on) used to refer to which Sunday after Pentecost a given Sunday may be through this season.

Rather than ordinary or "ho-hum," the idea of this season is to support disciples and the whole congregation in living out the gifts and callings discerned during Easter Season and commissioned on the Day of Pentecost. In the Northern Hemisphere, this season typically corresponds with "summer," when schools are out, and wide varieties of vacation schedules may mean the ability to coordinate or even operate some ministries in the congregation (such as Sunday School or some choirs) may be challenged or curtailed until a relaunch in the fall. This scheduling situation makes it even more critical for congregations and individuals to make sure the profound formational and missional purposes of this season are not overlooked, but intentionally planned for.

If you are using *A Disciple's Journal*, chances are you are already intent on strengthening your own discipleship. Let me encourage you to take another step. Ask your pastor to work with you to gather others who will take these months as an intentional journey of accountable discipleship and growth in ministry with you. Your congregation may not be able to provide a "program" for everyone who does this, but your pastor can certainly help you gather a "coalition of the willing" who will.

As you do, keep in mind that with the exceptions of Trinity Sunday and Christ the King Sunday, which begin and end this season, and All Saints, which falls during it, the three major tracks of readings (Old Testament, Epistle, and Gospel) are all "semi-continuous" during this season. None is intended to relate to the other, except for the "Bookend Sundays" and All Saints. The Old Testament readings are selections from the stories of the prophets, kings and patriarchs/matriarchs (depending on the year). The Epistle readings explore the meaning and practice of the Christian life, in particular early Christian communities. And the Gospel readings take us on a journey through the ministry and teaching of Jesus.

As suggested for the Season after Epiphany, you may wish to coordinate the way you and your group focus your energy and attention on the daily readings through these months with the particular stream of texts your congregation's worship leaders focus on during this time as a means to help reinforce the themes of the Sunday readings with your daily discipleship and ministry through these months.

Rev. Taylor Burton-Edwards

Trinity Sunday

Preparation for Sunday
Daily: Psalm 29

Thursday
Isaiah 1:1-4, 16-20
Romans 8:1-8

Friday
Isaiah 2:1-5
Romans 8:9-11

Saturday
Isaiah 5:15-24
John 15:18-20, 26-27

Sunday
Isaiah 6:1-8
Psalm 29
Romans 8:12-17
John 3:1-17

Reflection on Sunday
Daily: Psalm 20

Monday
Numbers 9:15-23
Revelation 4:1-8

Tuesday
Exodus 25:1-22
1 Corinthians 2:1-10

Wednesday
Numbers 6:22-27
Mark 4:21-25

The General Rule of Discipleship
To witness to Jesus Christ in the world and to follow his teachings
through acts of compassion, justice, worship, and devotion under the guidance of the Holy Spirit.

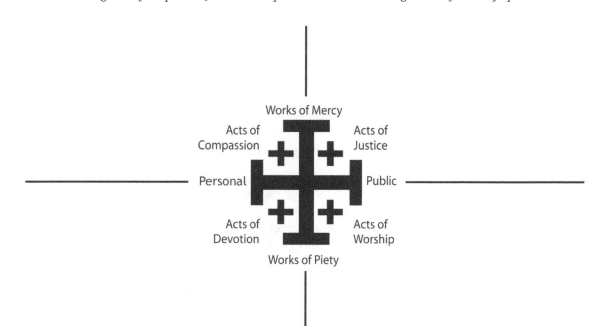

A Word from John Wesley

God worketh in you; therefore you must work: You must be "workers together with him," (they are the very words of the Apostle,) otherwise he will cease working. The general rule on which his gracious dispensations invariably proceed is this: "Unto him that hath shall be given; but from him that hath not,"—that does not improve the grace already given,—"shall be taken away what he assuredly hath." (So the words ought to be rendered.) Even St. Augustine, who is generally supposed to favour the contrary doctrine, makes that just remark, "He that made us without ourselves, will not save us without ourselves."

Sermon 85: "On Working Out Our Own Salvation," § III.7

A Hymn from Charles Wesley

A wonderful plurality
In the true God by faith we see,
Who hear the record of the Son
"I and my Father are but One;"
In different Persons we proclaim
On God eternally the same.

Father and Son in nature join,
Each Person is alike Divine:
Alike by heaven and earth adored,
Thy Spirit makes the glorious Third:
Co-equal, co-eternal Three,
Show thyself One, great God, in me.

(*Hymns on the Trinity*—1767, #18)

Prayers, Comments & Questions

Holy God, the earth is full of the glory of your love. May we your children, born of the Spirit, bear witness to your Son Jesus Christ, crucified and risen, that all the world may believe and have eternal life through the One who saves, Father, Son, and Holy Spirit, now and forever. Amen.

Sunday between May 24 and 28 inclusive
(if after Trinity Sunday)

Preparation for Sunday
Daily: Psalm 103:1-13, 22

Thursday
Ezekiel 16:1-14
Romans 3:1-8

Friday
Ezekiel 16:44-52
2 Peter 1:1-11

Saturday
Ezekiel 16:53-63
John 7:53—8:11

Sunday
Hosea 2:14-20
Psalm 103:1-13, 22
2 Corinthians 3:1-6
Mark 2:13-22

Reflection on Sunday
Daily: Psalm 45:6-17

Monday
Hosea 3:1-5
2 Corinthians 1:23—2:11

Tuesday
Hosea 14:1-9
2 Corinthians 11:1-15

Wednesday
Isaiah 62:1-5
John 3:22-36

The General Rule of Discipleship
To witness to Jesus Christ in the world and to follow his teachings
through acts of compassion, justice, worship, and devotion under the guidance of the Holy Spirit.

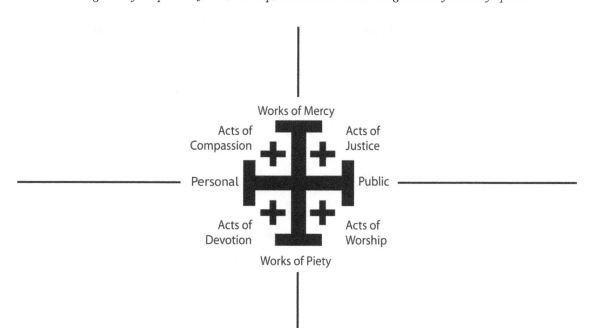

A Word from John Wesley

Presumption is one grand snare of the devil, in which many of the children of men are taken. They so presume upon the mercy of God as utterly to forget his justice. Although he has expressly declared, "Without holiness no man shall see the Lord," yet they flatter themselves, that in the end God will be better than his word. They imagine they may live and die in their sins, and nevertheless "escape the damnation of hell."

Sermon 86: "A Call to Backsliders," ¶ 1

A Hymn from Charles Wesley

Summoned my labour to renew,
And glad to act my part,
Lord, in thy name my work I do,
And with a single heart.

End of my every action thou,
In all things thee I see;
Accept my hallowed labour now;
I do it unto thee.

Whate'er the Father views as thine
He views with gracious eyes;
Jesu, this mean oblation join
To thy great sacrifice

(*Collection—1781*, #312:1-3)

Prayers, Comments & Questions

Your hand is upon your people, O God, to guide and protect them through the ages. Keep in your service those you have called and anointed, that the powers of this world may not overwhelm us, but that, secure in your love, we may carry out your will in the face of all adversity. Amen.

Sunday between May 29 and June 4 inclusive
(if after Trinity Sunday)

Preparation for Sunday
Daily: Psalm 139:1-6, 13-18

Thursday
1 Samuel 1:1-18
Acts 25:1-12

Friday
1 Samuel 1:19-27
Romans 8:31-39

Saturday
1 Samuel 2:1-10
John 7:19-24

Sunday
1 Samuel 3:1-20
Psalm 139:1-6, 13-18
2 Corinthians 4:5-12
Mark 2:23—3:6

Reflection on Sunday
Daily: Psalm 99

Monday
1 Samuel 2:11-17
Romans 9:19-29

Tuesday
1 Samuel 2:18-21
Acts 15:1-5, 22-35

Wednesday
1 Samuel 2:22-36
John 5:1-18

The General Rule of Discipleship
To witness to Jesus Christ in the world and to follow his teachings
through acts of compassion, justice, worship, and devotion under the guidance of the Holy Spirit.

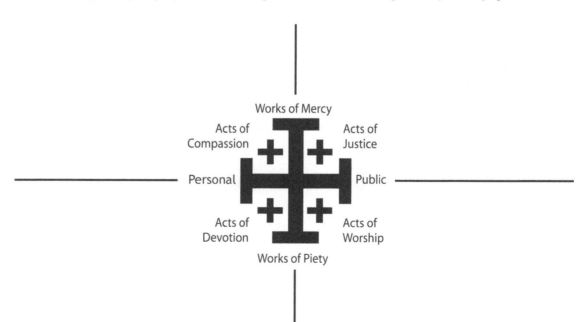

A Word from John Wesley

Riches, either desired or possessed, naturally lead to some or other of these foolish and hurtful desires; and by affording the means of gratifying them all, naturally tend to increase them. And there is a near connexion between unholy desires, and every other unholy passion and temper. We easily pass from these to pride, anger, bitterness, envy, malice, revengefulness; to an head-strong, unadvisable, unreprovable spirit: Indeed to every temper that is earthly, sensual, or devilish. All these the desire or possession of riches naturally tends to create, strengthen, and increase.

Sermon 87: "The Danger of Riches," § I.18

A Hymn from Charles Wesley

Now I have found the ground, wherein
Sure my soul's anchor may remain;
The wounds of Jesus, for my sin
Before the world's foundation slain:
Whose mercy shall unshaken stay
When heaven and earth are fled away.

Father, thine everlasting grace
Our scanty thought surpasses far;
Thy heart still melts with tenderness;
Thy arms of love still open are
Returning sinners to receive,
That mercy they may taste and live!

O love, thou bottomless abyss!
My sins are swallowed up in thee;
Covered is my unrighteousness,
Nor spot of guilt remains in me;
While Jesu's blood, through earth and skies,
Mercy, free, boundless mercy cries!

(*Collection—1781*, #182:1-3)

Prayers, Comments & Questions

Holy God, you search us out and know us better than we know ourselves. As Samuel looked to Eli for help to discern your voice and as the disciples looked to Jesus for your wisdom on the Sabbath, so raise up in our day faithful servants who will speak your word to us with clarity and grace, with justice and true compassion. We pray through Christ, the Word made flesh. Amen.

Sunday between June 5 and 11 inclusive
(if after Trinity Sunday)

Preparation for Sunday
Daily: Psalm 138

Thursday
1 Samuel 4:1-22
1 Peter 4:7-19

Friday
1 Samuel 5:1-12
2 Corinthians 5:1-5

Saturday
1 Samuel 6:1-18
Luke 8:4-15

Sunday
1 Samuel 8:4-20; 11:14-15
Psalm 138
2 Corinthians 4:13—5:1
Mark 3:20-35

Reflection on Sunday
Daily: Psalm 108

Monday
1 Samuel 7:3-15
Revelation 20:1-6

Tuesday
1 Samuel 8:1-22
Revelation 20:7-15

Wednesday
1 Samuel 9:1-14
Luke 11:14-28

The General Rule of Discipleship
To witness to Jesus Christ in the world and to follow his teachings
through acts of compassion, justice, worship, and devotion under the guidance of the Holy Spirit.

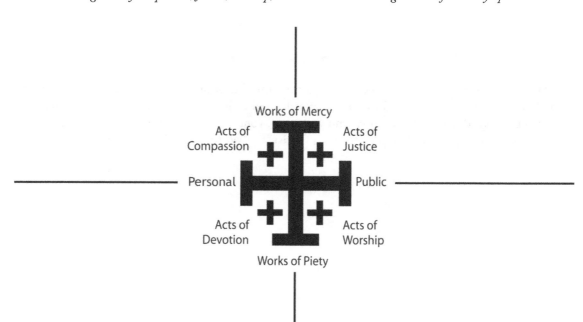

A Word from John Wesley

I ask, then, in the name of God, Who of you "desire to be rich:" Which of you (ask your own hearts in the sight of God) seriously and deliberately desire (and perhaps applaud your-selves for so doing, as no small instance of your prudence) to have more than food to eat, and raiment to put on, and a house to cover you. Who of you desires to have more than the plain necessaries and conveniences of life? Stop! Consider! What are you doing Evil is before you! Will you rush upon the point of a sword By the grace of God, turn and live!

Sermon 87: "The Danger of Riches," §II.2

A Hymn from Charles Wesley

Now I have found the ground, wherein
Sure my soul's anchor may remain;
The wounds of Jesus, for my sin
Before the world's foundation slain:
Whose mercy shall unshaken stay
When heaven and earth are fled away.

Father, thine everlasting grace
Our scanty thought surpasses far;
Thy heart still melts with tenderness;
Thy arms of love still open are
Returning sinners to receive,
That mercy they may taste and live!

O love, thou bottomless abyss!
My sins are swallowed up in thee;
Covered is my unrighteousness,
Nor spot of guilt remains in me;
While Jesu's blood, through earth and skies,
Mercy, free, boundless mercy cries!

(*Collection—1781*, #182:1-3)

Prayers, Comments & Questions

Unlike earthly kings, you, O Lord, are ever steadfast and faithful. You sent us your Son, Jesus the Christ, to rule over us, not as a tyrant, but as a gentle shepherd. Keep us united and strong in faith, that we may always know your presence in our lives; and, when you call us home, may we enter your heavenly kingdom where you live and reign forever and ever. Amen.

Sunday between June 12 and 18 inclusive
(if after Trinity Sunday)

Preparation for Sunday
Daily: Psalm 20

Thursday
1 Samuel 9:15-27
Hebrews 2:5-9

Friday
1 Samuel 10:1-8
Hebrews 11:4-7

Saturday
1 Samuel 13:1-15a
Mark 4:1-20

Sunday
1 Samuel 15:34—16:13
Psalm 20
2 Corinthians 5:6-17
Mark 4:26-34

Reflection on Sunday
Daily: Psalm 53

Monday
1 Samuel 13:23—14:23
Galatians 6:11-18

Tuesday
1 Samuel 15:10-23
Revelation 21:22—22:5

Wednesday
1 Samuel 15:24-31
Luke 6:43-45

The General Rule of Discipleship
To witness to Jesus Christ in the world and to follow his teachings
through acts of compassion, justice, worship, and devotion under the guidance of the Holy Spirit.

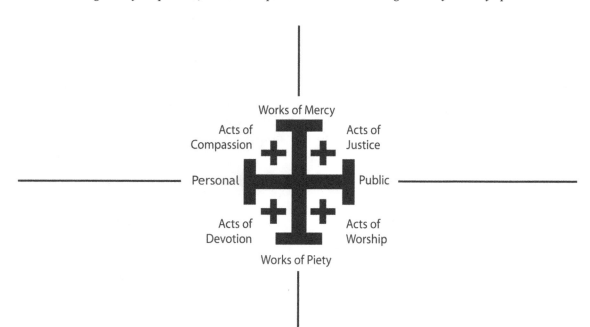

A Word from John Wesley

O ye lovers of money, hear the word of the Lord! Suppose ye that money, though multiplied as the sand of the sea, can give happiness. Then you are "given up to a strong delusion, to believe a lie;"—a palpable lie, confuted daily by a thousand experiments. Open your eyes! Look all around you! Are the richest men the happiest? Have those the largest share of content who have the largest possessions? Is not the very reverse true? Is it not a common observation, that the richest of men are, in general, the most discontented, the most miserable? Had not the far greater part of them more content when they had less money? Look into your breasts. If you are increased in goods, are you proportionably increased in happiness? You have more substance; but have you more content? You know that in seeking happiness from riches, you are only striving to drink out of empty cups. And let them be painted and gilded ever so finely, they are empty still.

Sermon 87: "The Danger of Riches," §II.10

A Hymn from Charles Wesley

When darkness intercepts the skies,
And sorrow's waves around me roll,
When high the storms of passion rise,
And half o'erwhelm my sinking soul,
My soul a sudden calm shall feel,
And hear a whisper, 'Peace, be still!'

Though in affliction's furnace tried,
Unhurt on snares and deaths I'll tread;
Though sin assail, and hell thrown wide
Pour all its flames upon my head,
Like Moses' bush I'll mount the higher,
And flourish unconsumed in fire.

(*Collection—1781*, #264:6 & 7)

Prayers, Comments & Questions

Mighty God, to you belong the mysteries of the universe. You transform shepherds into kings, the smallest seeds into magnificent trees, and hardened hearts into loving ones. Bless us with your life-giving Spirit; re-create us in your image; and shape us to your purposes, through Jesus Christ. Amen.

Sunday between June 19 and 25 inclusive
(if after Trinity Sunday)

Preparation for Sunday
Daily: Psalm 9:9-20

Thursday
1 Samuel 16:14-23
Acts 20:1-16

Friday
1 Samuel 17:55—18:5
Acts 21:1-16

Saturday
1 Samuel 18:1-4
Luke 21:25-28

Sunday
1 Samuel 17:32-49
Psalm 9:9-20
2 Corinthians 6:1-13
Mark 4:35-41

Reflection on Sunday
Daily: Psalm 119:113-128

Monday
1 Samuel 18:6-30
Acts 27:13-38

Tuesday
1 Samuel 19:1-7
Acts 27:39-44

Wednesday
1 Samuel 19:8-17
Mark 6:45-52

The General Rule of Discipleship
To witness to Jesus Christ in the world and to follow his teachings
through acts of compassion, justice, worship, and devotion under the guidance of the Holy Spirit.

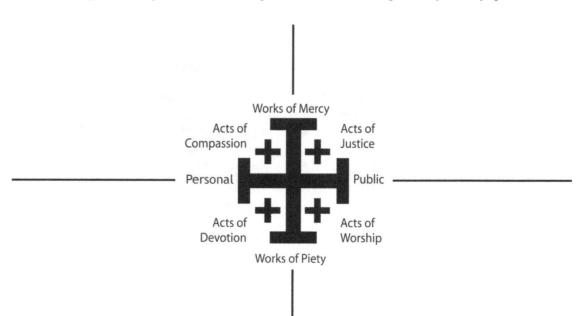

A Word from John Wesley

The wearing gay or costly apparel naturally tends to breed and to increase vanity. By vanity I here mean, the love and desire of being admired and praised. Every one of you that is fond of dress has a witness of this in your own bosom. Whether you will confess it before man or no, you are convinced of this before God. You know in your hearts, it is with a view to be admired that you thus adorn yourselves; and that you would not be at the pains were none to see you but God and his holy angels. Now, the more you indulge this foolish desire, the more it grows upon you. You have vanity enough by nature; but by thus indulging it, you increase it a hundred-fold. O stop! Aim at pleasing God alone, and all these ornaments will drop off.

Sermon 88: "On Dress," ¶ 11

A Hymn from Charles Wesley

Come, O my guilty brethren, come,
Groaning beneath your load of sin;
His bleeding heart shall make you room,
His open side shall take you in.
He calls you now, invites you home—
Come, O my guilty brethren, come.

For you the purple current flowed
In pardons from his wounded side;
Languished for you th'eternal God,
For you the Prince of glory died.
Believe, and all your sin's forgiven,
Only believe—and yours is heaven!

(*Collection—1781*, #29:6 & 7)

Prayers, Comments & Questions

God our protector, you stood by David in the time of trial. Stand with us through all life's storms, giving us courage to risk danger to protect those who are oppressed and poor, that they may know you as their stronghold and hope. Amen.

Sunday between June 26 and July 2 inclusive

Preparation for Sunday
Daily: Psalm 130

Thursday
1 Samuel 19:18-24
2 Corinthians 7:2-16

Friday
1 Samuel 20:1-25
2 Corinthians 8:1-7

Saturday
1 Samuel 20:27-42
Luke 4:31-37

Sunday
2 Samuel 1:1, 17-27
Psalm 130
2 Corinthians 8:7-15
Mark 5:21-43

Reflection on Sunday
Daily: Psalm 18:1-6, 43-50

Monday
1 Samuel 23:14-18
2 Corinthians 8:16-24

Tuesday
1 Samuel 31:1-13
2 Corinthians 9:1-5

Wednesday
1 Chronicles 10:1-14
Mark 9:14-29

The General Rule of Discipleship
To witness to Jesus Christ in the world and to follow his teachings
through acts of compassion, justice, worship, and devotion under the guidance of the Holy Spirit.

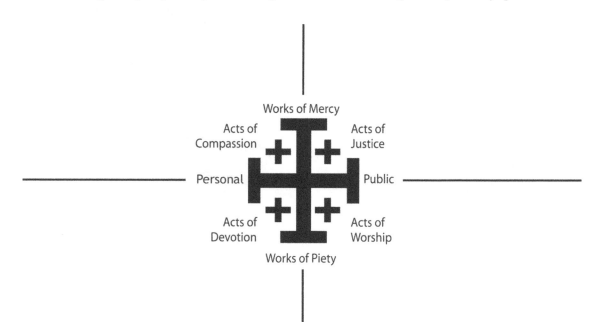

A Word from John Wesley

The wearing costly array is directly opposite to the being adorned with good works. Nothing can be more evident than this; for the more you lay out on your own apparel, the less you have left to clothe the naked, to feed the hungry, to lodge the strangers, to relieve those that are sick and in prison, and to lessen the numberless afflictions to which we are exposed in this vale of tears. And here is no room for the evasion used before: "I may be as humble in cloth of gold, as in sackcloth." If you could be as humble when you choose costly as when you choose plain apparel, (which I flatly deny,) yet you could not be as beneficent,—as plenteous in good works. Every shilling which you save from your own apparel, you may expend in clothing the naked, and relieving the various necessities of the poor, whom ye "have always with you." Therefore, every shilling which you needlessly spend on your apparel is, in effect, stolen from God and the poor!

Sermon 88: "On Dress," ¶ 14

A Hymn from Charles Wesley

What though my shrinking flesh complain
And murmur to contend so long?
I rise superior to my pain:
When I am weak, then I am strong;
And when my all of strength shall fail
I shall with the God-man prevail.

Yield to me now—for I am weak,
But confident in self-despair!
Speak to my heart, in blessings speak,
Be conquered by my instant prayer:
Speak, or thou never hence shalt move,
And tell me if thy name is LOVE.

(*Collection—1781*, #136:5 & 6)

Prayers, Comments & Questions

God of hope, you are ruler of night as well as day, guardian of those who wander in the shadows. Be new light of life for those who live in the darkness of despair, for prisoners of guilt and grief, for victims of fantasy and depression, that even where death's cold grip tightens, we may know the power of the one who conquered fear and death. Amen.

Sunday between July 3 and 9 inclusive

Preparation for Sunday
Daily: Psalm 48

Thursday
2 Samuel 2:1-11
1 Corinthians 4:8-13

Friday
2 Samuel 3:1-12
2 Corinthians 10:7-10

Saturday
2 Samuel 3:31-38
Matthew 8:18-22

Sunday
2 Samuel 5:1-5, 9-10
Psalm 48
2 Corinthians 12:2-10
Mark 6:1-13

Reflection on Sunday
Daily: Psalm 21

Monday
2 Samuel 5:1-10
2 Corinthians 11:16-33

Tuesday
2 Samuel 5:11-16
James 5:7-12

Wednesday
2 Samuel 5:17-25
John 7:1-9

The General Rule of Discipleship
To witness to Jesus Christ in the world and to follow his teachings
through acts of compassion, justice, worship, and devotion under the guidance of the Holy Spirit.

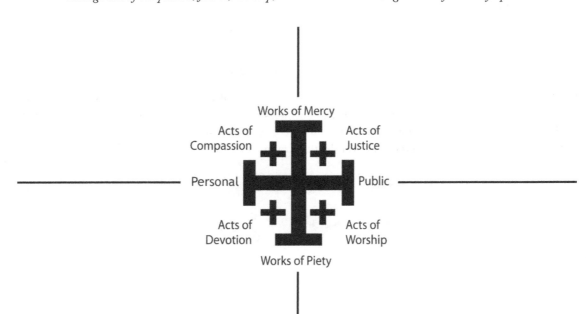

A Word from John Wesley

In what spirit do you go through your business In the spirit of the world, or the Spirit of Christ I am afraid thousands of those who are called good Christians do not understand the question. If you act in the Spirit of Christ you carry the end you at first proposed through all your work from first to last. You do everything in the spirit of sacrifice, giving up your will to the will of God; and continually aiming, not at ease, pleasure, or riches; not at anything "this short enduring world can give;" but merely at the glory of God. Now can anyone deny that this is the most excellent way of pursuing worldly business?

Sermon 89: "The More Excellent Way" § III.3

A Hymn from Charles Wesley

Prophet, to me reveal
Thy Father's perfect will:
Never mortal spake like thee,
Human prophet like divine;
Loud and strong their voices be,
Small, and still, and inward thine!

On thee my Priest I call,
Thy blood atoned for all:
Still the Lamb as slain appears,
Still thou stand'st before the throne,
Ever off'ring up my prayers,
These presenting with thy own.

Jesu, thou art my King,
From thee my strength I bring:
Shadowed by thy mighty hand,
Saviour, who shall pluck me thence?
Faith supports, by faith I stand,
Strong as thy omnipotence.

(*Collection—1781*, #186:6-8)

Prayers, Comments & Questions

Guardian of the weak, through the teachings of your prophets you have claimed our cities, towns, and homes as temples of your presence and citadels of your justice. Turn the places we live into strongholds of your grace, that the most vulnerable as well as the most powerful among us may find peace in the security that comes in the strong name of Jesus Christ. Amen.

Sunday between July 10 and 16 inclusive

Preparation for Sunday
Daily: Psalm 24

Thursday
Exodus 25:10-22
Colossians 2:1-5

Friday
Exodus 37:1-16
Colossians 4:2-18

Saturday
Numbers 10:11-36
Luke 1:57-80

Sunday
2 Samuel 6:1-5, 12b-19
Psalm 24
Ephesians 1:3-14
Mark 6:14-29

Reflection on Sunday
Daily: Psalm 68:24-35

Monday
2 Samuel 6:6-12a
Acts 21:27-39

Tuesday
2 Samuel 3:12-16
Acts 23:12-35

Wednesday
2 Samuel 6:16-23
Luke 7:31-35

The General Rule of Discipleship
*To witness to Jesus Christ in the world and to follow his teachings
through acts of compassion, justice, worship, and devotion under the guidance of the Holy Spirit.*

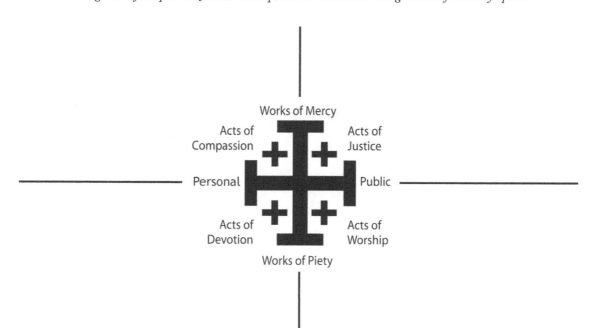

A Word from John Wesley

"Love is not puffed up." As is the measure of love, so is the measure of humility. Nothing humbles the soul so deeply as love: It casts out all "high conceits, engendering pride;" all arrogance and overweaning; makes us little, and poor, and base, and vile in our own eyes. It abases us both before God and man; makes us willing to be the least of all, and the servants of all, and teaches us to say, "A mote in the sun-beam is little, but I am infinitely less in the presence of God."

Sermon 91: "On Charity," § I.4

A Hymn from Charles Wesley

Regard me with a gracious eye,
The long-sought blessing give,
And bid me, at the point to die,
Behold thy face and live.

A darker soul did never yet
Thy promised help implore;
O, that I now my Lord might meet,
And never lose him more!

Now, Jesus, now the Father's love
Shed in my heart abroad,
The middle wall of sin remove,
And let me into God!

(*Collection—1781*, #113:4-6)

Prayers, Comments & Questions

God of Hosts, before whom David danced and sang, Mother of Mercy and Father of our Lord Jesus Christ, in whom all things cohere: Whenever we are confronted by lust, hate, or fear, give us the faith of John the baptizer, that we may trust in the redemption of your Messiah. Amen.

Sunday between July 17 and 23 inclusive

Preparation for Sunday
Daily: Psalm 89:20-37

Thursday
1 Chronicles 11:15-19
Colossians 1:15-23

Friday
1 Chronicles 14:1-2
Acts 17:16-31

Saturday
1 Chronicles 15:1-2,
    16:4-13
Luke 18:35-43

Sunday
2 Samuel 7:1-14a
Psalm 89:20-37
Ephesians 2:11-22
Mark 6:30-34, 53-56

Reflection on Sunday
Daily: Psalm 61

Monday
2 Samuel 7:18-29
Hebrews 13:17-25

Tuesday
2 Samuel 8:1-18
Acts 20:17-38

Wednesday
2 Samuel 9:1-13
Luke 15:1-7

The General Rule of Discipleship
To witness to Jesus Christ in the world and to follow his teachings
through acts of compassion, justice, worship, and devotion under the guidance of the Holy Spirit.

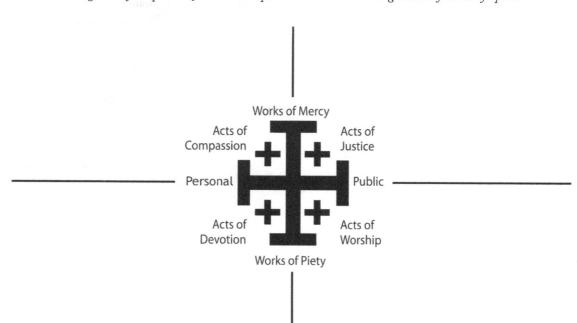

A Word from John Wesley

Certainly he who is full of love is "gentle towards all men." He "in meekness instructs those that oppose themselves;" that oppose what he loves most, even the truth of God, or that holiness without which no man shall see the Lord: Not knowing but "God, peradventure, may bring them to the knowledge of the truth." However provoked, he does "not return evil for evil, or railing for railing." Yea, he "blesses those that curse him, and does good to them that despitefully use him and persecute him." He "is not overcome of evil, but" always "overcomes evil with good."

Sermon 91: "On Charity," § I.7

A Hymn from Charles Wesley

Holy Lamb, who thee confess,
Followers of thy holiness,
Thee they ever keep in view,
Ever ask, 'What shall we do?'

Governed by thy only will,
All thy words we would fulfil,
Would in all thy footsteps go,
Walk as Jesus walked below.

While thou didst on earth appear,
Servant to thy servants here,
Mindful of thy place above,
All thy life was prayer and love.

(*Collection—1781*, #515:1-3)

Prayers, Comments & Questions

Holy God of Israel, ever present and moving among your people, draw us near to you, that in place of hostility there may be peace; in place of loneliness, compassion; in place of aimlessness, direction; and in place of sickness, healing; through Christ Jesus, in whom you draw near to us. Amen.

Sunday between July 24 and 30 inclusive

Preparation for Sunday
Daily: Psalm 14

Thursday
2 Samuel 10:1-5
Colossians 1:9-14

Friday
2 Samuel 10:6-12
Colossians 3:12-17

Saturday
2 Samuel 10:13-19
John 4:31-38

Sunday
2 Samuel 11:1-15
Psalm 14
Ephesians 3:14-21
John 6:1-21

Reflection on Sunday
Daily: Psalm 37:12-22

Monday
2 Samuel 11:14-21
Philippians 4:10-20

Tuesday
2 Samuel 11:22-27
Romans 15:22-33

Wednesday
2 Chronicles 9:29-31
Mark 6:35-44

The General Rule of Discipleship
To witness to Jesus Christ in the world and to follow his teachings
through acts of compassion, justice, worship, and devotion under the guidance of the Holy Spirit.

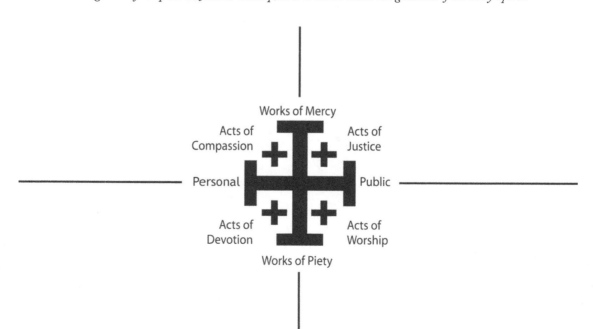

A Word from John Wesley

"Love is longsuffering." It endures not a few affronts, reproaches, injuries; but all things, which God is pleased to permit either men or devils to inflict. It arms the soul with inviolable patience; not harsh stoical patience, but yielding as the air, which, making no resistance to the stroke, receives no harm thereby. The lover of mankind remembers Him who suffered for us, "leaving us an example that we might tread in his steps." Accordingly, "if his enemy hunger, he feeds him; if he thirst, he gives him drink:" And by so doing, he "heaps coals of fire," of melting love, upon his head. "And many waters cannot quench this love; neither can the floods" of ingratitude "drown it."

Sermon 91: "On Charity," § I.8

A Hymn from Charles Wesley

Christ, my Master and my Lord,
Let me thy forerunner be;
O be mindful of thy word,
Visit them, and visit me!
To this house, and all herein,
Now let thy salvation come!
Save our souls from inbred sin,
Make us thy eternal home!

Let us never, never rest
Till the promise is fulfilled;
Till we are of thee possessed,
Pardoned, sanctified, and sealed;
Till we all, in love renewed,
Find the pearl that Adam lost,
Temples of the living God,
Father, Son, and Holy Ghost.

(*Collection—1781*, #467:2 & 3)

Prayers, Comments & Questions

In your compassionate love, O God, you nourish us with the words of life and bread of blessing. Grant that Jesus may calm our fears and move our hearts to praise your goodness by sharing our bread with others. Amen.

Sunday between July 31 and August 6 inclusive

Preparation for Sunday
Daily: Psalm 51:1-12

Thursday
Exodus 32:19-26a
1 Corinthians 11:17-22

Friday
Joshua 23:1-16
1 Corinthians 11:27-34

Saturday
Judges 6:1-10
Matthew 16:5-12

Sunday
2 Samuel 11:26—12:13a
Psalm 51:1-12
Ephesians 4:1-16
John 6:24-35

Reflection on Sunday
Daily: Psalm 50:16-23

Monday
2 Samuel 12:15-25
Ephesians 4:17-24

Tuesday
2 Samuel 13:1-19
1 Corinthians 12:27-31

Wednesday
2 Samuel 13:20-36
Mark 8:1-10

The General Rule of Discipleship
To witness to Jesus Christ in the world and to follow his teachings
through acts of compassion, justice, worship, and devotion under the guidance of the Holy Spirit.

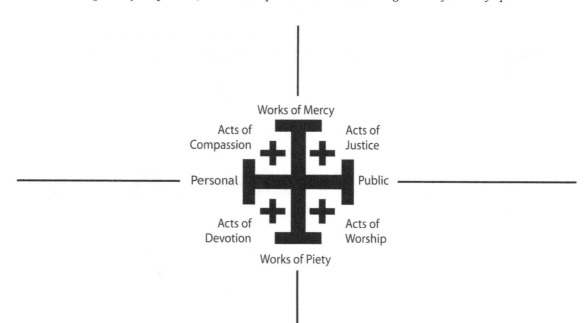

A Word from John Wesley

"And though I have all faith, so that I could remove mountains."—The faith which is able to do this cannot be the fruit of vain imagination, a mere madman's dream, a system of opinions; but must be a real work of God: Otherwise it could not have such an effect. Yet if this faith does not work by love, if it does not produce universal holiness, if it does not bring forth lowliness, meekness, and resignation, it will profit me nothing. This is as certain a truth as any that is delivered in the whole oracles of God. All faith that is, that ever was, or ever can be, separate from tender benevolence to every child of man, friend or foe, Christian, Jew, Heretic, or Pagan,—separate from gentleness to all men; separate from resignation in all events, and contentedness in all conditions,—is not the faith of a Christian, and will stand us in no stead before the face of God.

Sermon 91: "On Charity," § III.6

A Hymn from Charles Wesley

Give me, Lord, the victory,
My heart's desire fulfil;
Let it now be done to me
According to thy will!
Give me living bread to eat,
And say, in answer to my call,
Canaanite, thy faith is great!
My grace is free for all.

If thy grace for all is free,
Thy call now let me hear;
Show this token upon me,
And bring salvation near.
Now the gracious word repeat,
The word of healing to my soul:
Canaanite, thy faith is great!
Thy faith hath made thee whole.

(*Collection—1781*, #158:5 & 6)

Prayers, Comments & Questions

God of the lowly and the mighty, you know the ugliness of your people when we harm and destroy one another, yet you offer us forgiveness of our sins if we but turn to you. Expand our hearts to receive the mercy you give us, that, in turn, we may share your grace and mercy with others each moment of our lives. Amen.

Sunday between August 7 and 13 inclusive

Preparation for Sunday
Daily: Psalm 130

Thursday
2 Samuel 13:37—14:24
Romans 15:1-6

Friday
2 Samuel 14:25-33
Galatians 6:1-10

Saturday
2 Samuel 15:1-13
Matthew 7:7-11

Sunday
2 Samuel 18:5-9, 15, 31-33
Psalm 130
Ephesians 4:25—5:2
John 6:35, 41-51

Reflection on Sunday
Daily: Psalm 57

Monday
2 Samuel 15:13-31
Ephesians 5:1-14

Tuesday
2 Samuel 18:19-33
2 Peter 3:14-18

Wednesday
2 Samuel 19:1-18
John 6:35-40

The General Rule of Discipleship
To witness to Jesus Christ in the world and to follow his teachings
through acts of compassion, justice, worship, and devotion under the guidance of the Holy Spirit.

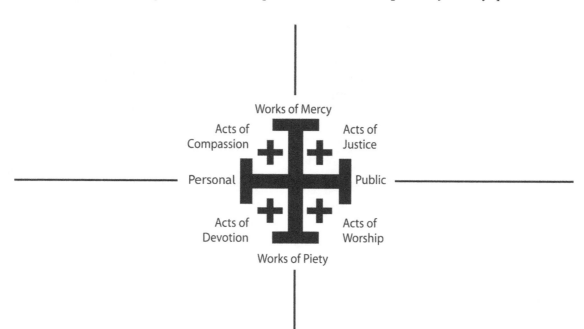

A Word from John Wesley

From hence it follows, that the properties of love are the properties of zeal also. Now, one of the chief properties of love is humility: "Love is not puffed up." Accordingly, this is a property of true zeal: humility is inseparable from it. As is the degree of zeal, such is the degree of humility: they must rise and fall together. The same love which fills a man with zeal for God, makes him little, and poor, and vile in his own eyes.

Sermon 92: "On Zeal," § II.2

A Hymn from Charles Wesley

Lay thy weighty cross on me,
All my unbelief control;
Till the rebel cease to be
Keep him down within my soul;
That he never more may move,
Root and ground me fast in love.

Give me faith to hold me up,
Walking over life's rough sea;
Holy, purifying hope
Still my soul's sure anchor be;
That I may be always thine,
Perfect me in love divine.

(*Collection—1781*, #176:3 & 4)

Prayers, Comments & Questions

Bread of heaven, you feed us in the depths of grief, sin, and hostility. Nourish us with your word through the long hours of tears and in the dawning awareness of our need for forgiveness, so that we may be redeemed by your steadfast love. Amen.

Sunday between August 14 and 20 inclusive

Preparation for Sunday
Daily: Psalm 111

Thursday
1 Kings 1:1-30
Acts 6:8-15

Friday
1 Kings 1:28-48
Romans 16:17-20

Saturday
1 Kings 2:1-11
John 4:7-26

Sunday
1 Kings 2:10-12; 3:3-14
Psalm 111
Ephesians 5:15-20
John 6:51-58

Reflection on Sunday
Daily: Psalm 101

Monday
1 Kings 3:16-28
Acts 6:1-7

Tuesday
1 Kings 7:1-12
Acts 7:9-16

Wednesday
1 Kings 8:1-21
Mark 8:14-21

The General Rule of Discipleship
To witness to Jesus Christ in the world and to follow his teachings
through acts of compassion, justice, worship, and devotion under the guidance of the Holy Spirit.

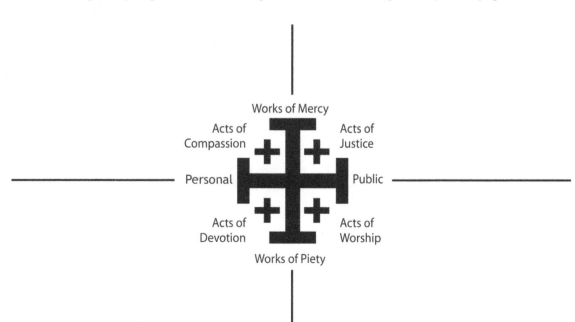

A Word from John Wesley

Another of the properties of love is meekness: consequently, it is one of the properties of zeal. It teaches us to be meek, as well as lowly; to be equally superior to anger or pride. Like as the wax melteth at the fire, so before this sacred flame all turbulent passions melt away, and leave the soul unruffled and serene.

Sermon 92: "On Zeal," § II.2

A Hymn from Charles Wesley

Lord, regard my earnest cry,
A potsherd of the earth,
A poor, guilty worm am I,
A Canaanite by birth.
Save me from this tyranny,
From all the power of Satan save;
Mercy, mercy upon me,
Thou Son of David, have!

To the sheep of Israel's fold
Thou in thy flesh wast sent;
Yet the Gentiles now behold
In thee their covenant.
See me then, with pity see,
A sinner whom thou cam'st to save!
Mercy, mercy, upon me,
Thou Son of David, have!

(*Collection—1781*, #158:1 & 2)

Prayers, Comments & Questions

Living God, you are the giver of wisdom and true discernment, guiding those who seek your ways to choose the good. Mercifully grant that your people, feasting on the true bread of heaven, may have eternal life in Jesus Christ our Lord. Amen.

Sunday between August 21 and 27 inclusive

Preparation for Sunday
Daily: Psalm 84

Thursday
1 Kings 4:20-28
1 Thessalonians 5:1-11

Friday
1 Kings 4:29-34
Romans 13:11-14

Saturday
1 Kings 5:1-12
Luke 11:5-13

Sunday
1 Kings 8:22-30, 41-43
Psalm 84
Ephesians 6:10-20
John 6:56-69

Reflection on Sunday
Daily: Psalm 11

Monday
1 Kings 5:13-18
Ephesians 5:21—6:9

Tuesday
1 Kings 6:1-14
Ephesians 6:21-24

Wednesday
1 Kings 6:15-38
John 15:16-25

The General Rule of Discipleship
To witness to Jesus Christ in the world and to follow his teachings
through acts of compassion, justice, worship, and devotion under the guidance of the Holy Spirit.

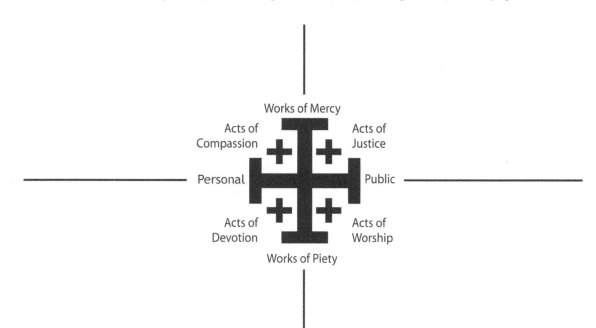

A Word from John Wesley

Yet another property of love, and consequently of zeal, is unwearied patience: for "love endureth all things." It arms the soul with entire resignation to all the disposals of divine Providence, and teaches us to say, in every occurrence, "It is the Lord; let him do what seemeth him good." It enables us, in whatever state, therewith to be content; to repine at nothing, to murmur at nothing, "but in every thing to give thanks."

Sermon 92: "On Zeal," § II.3

A Hymn from Charles Wesley

How happy then are we,
Who build, O Lord, on thee!
What can our foundation shock?
Though the shattered earth remove,
Stands our city on a rock,
On the rock of heavenly love.

A house we call our own,
Which cannot be o'erthrown:
In the general ruin sure,
Storms and earthquakes it defies,
Built immovably secure,
Built eternal in the skies.

(*Collection—1781*, #65:2 & 3)

Prayers, Comments & Questions

Gracious God, although we once were strangers, you receive us as friends and draw us home to you. Set your living bread before us that, feasting around your table, we may be strengthened to continue the work to which your Son commissioned us. Amen.

Sunday between August 28 and September 3 inclusive

Preparation for Sunday
Daily: Psalm 45:1-2, 6-9

Thursday
Song of Solomon 1:1-17
James 1:1-8

Friday
Song of Solomon 2:1-7
James 1:9-16

Saturday
Hosea 3:1-5
John 18:28-32

Sunday
Song of Solomon 2:8-13
Psalm 45:1-2, 6-9
James 1:17-27
Mark 7:1-8, 14-15, 21-23

Reflection on Sunday
Daily: Psalm 144:9-15

Monday
Song of Solomon 3:6-11
1 Timothy 4:6-16

Tuesday
Song of Solomon 5:2—6:3
1 Peter 2:19-25

Wednesday
Song of Solomon 8:5-7
Mark 7:9-23

The General Rule of Discipleship
To witness to Jesus Christ in the world and to follow his teachings
through acts of compassion, justice, worship, and devotion under the guidance of the Holy Spirit.

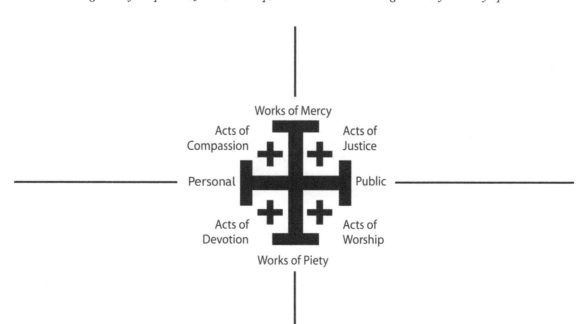

A Word from John Wesley

There is a Fourth property of Christian zeal, which deserves to be more particularly considered. This we learn from the very words of the Apostle, "It is good to be jealously affected always" (not to have transient touches of zeal, but a steady, rooted disposition) "in a good thing: "in that which is good: for the proper object of zeal is, good in general; that is, everything that is good, really such, in the sight of God."

Sermon 92: "On Zeal," § II.4

A Hymn from Charles Wesley

Pain and sickness, at thy word,
And sin and sorrow flies;
Speak to me, Almighty Lord,
And bid my spirit rise!
Bid me take my burden up,
The bed on which thyself didst lie,
When on Calvary's steep top
My Jesus deigned to die.

Bid me bear the hallowed cross
Which thou hast borne before,
Walk in all thy righteous laws,
And go, and sin no more.
Jesus, I on thee alone
For persevering grace depend!
Love me freely, love thine own,
And love me to the end!

(*Collection—1781*, #160:6 & 7)

Prayers, Comments & Questions

Blessed are you, O Lord and Lover, source of beauty and depth of passion. Strengthen and inspire us to do the word we hear and live the faith we confess. Amen.

Sunday between September 4 and 10 inclusive

Preparation for Sunday
Daily: Psalm 125

Thursday
Proverbs 1:1-9
Romans 2:1-11

Friday
Proverbs 4:10-27
Romans 2:12-16

Saturday
Proverbs 8:1-31
Matthews 15:21-31

Sunday
Proverbs 22:1-2, 8-9, 22-23
Psalm 125
James 2:1-17
Mark 7:24-37

Reflection on Sunday
Daily: Psalm 73:1-20

Monday
Proverbs 8:32—9:6
Hebrews 11:29—12:2

Tuesday
Proverbs 11:1-31
Hebrews 12:3-13

Wednesday
Proverbs 14:1-9
Matthew 17:14-21

The General Rule of Discipleship
To witness to Jesus Christ in the world and to follow his teachings
through acts of compassion, justice, worship, and devotion under the guidance of the Holy Spirit.

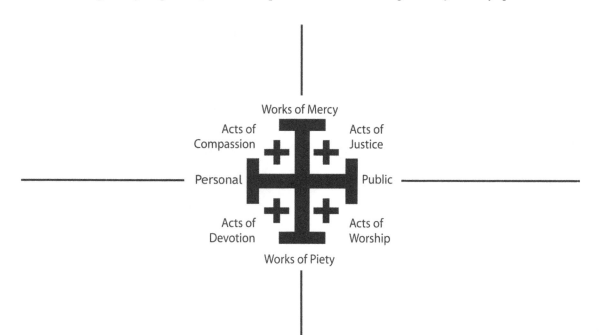

A Word from John Wesley

In a Christian believer love sits upon the throne which is erected in the inmost soul; namely, love of God and man, which fills the whole heart, and reigns without a rival. In a circle near the throne are all holy tempers; - longsuffering, gentleness, meekness, fidelity, temperance; and if any other were comprised in "the mind which was in Christ Jesus." In an exterior circle are all the works of mercy, whether to the souls or bodies of men. By these we exercise all holy tempers—by these we continually improve them, so that all these are real means of grace, although this is not commonly adverted to. Next to these are those that are usually termed works of piety—reading and hearing the word, public, family, private prayer, receiving the Lord's supper, fasting or abstinence. Lastly, that his followers may the more effectually provoke one another to love, holy tempers, and good works, our blessed Lord has united them together in one body, the church, dispersed all over the earth—a little emblem of which, of the church universal, we have in every particular Christian congregation.

Sermon 92: "On Zeal," § II.5

A Hymn from Charles Wesley

Eternal Wisdom, thee we praise,
Thee the creation sings;
With thy loud name, rocks, hills, and seas,
And heaven's high palace rings.

Thy hand, how wide it spreads the sky!
How glorious to behold!
Tinged with a blue of heavenly dye,
And starred with sparkling gold.

There thou hast bid the globes of light
Their endless circles run;
There the pale planet rules the night,
The day obeys the sun.

If down I turn my wond'ring eyes
On clouds and storms below,
Those under-regions of the skies
Thy num'rous glories show.

(*Collection—1781*, #217:1-4)

Prayers, Comments & Questions

Holy Lord, maker of us all, you call us to love our neighbors as ourselves and teach us that faith without works is dead. Open us to the opportunities for ministry that lie before us, where faith and works and the need of our neighbor come together in the name of Jesus Christ, our Savior. Amen.

Sunday between September 11 and 17 inclusive

Preparation for Sunday
Daily: Psalm 19

Thursday
Proverbs 15:1-17
Hebrews 11:17-22

Friday
Proverbs 19:24-29
James 2:17-26

Saturday
Proverbs 21:1-17
Matthew 21:23-32

Sunday
Proverbs 1:20-33
Psalm 19
James 3:1-12
Mark 8:27-38

Reflection on Sunday
Daily: Psalm 73:21-28

Monday
Proverbs 22:1-21
Romans 3:9-20

Tuesday
Proverbs 25:1-28
Colossians 3:1-11

Wednesday
Proverbs 29:1-27
John 7:25-36

The General Rule of Discipleship
To witness to Jesus Christ in the world and to follow his teachings
through acts of compassion, justice, worship, and devotion under the guidance of the Holy Spirit.

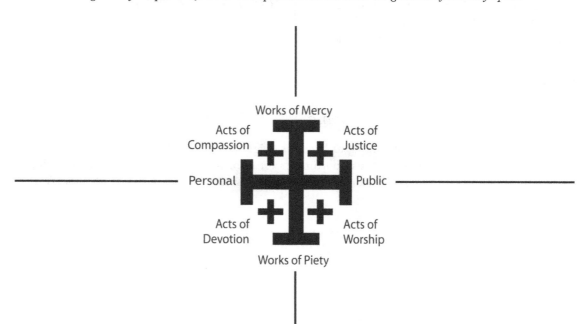

A Word from John Wesley

Every Christian ought, undoubtedly, to be zealous for the church, bearing a strong affection to it, and earnestly desiring its prosperity and increase. He ought to be thus zealous, as for the church universal, praying for it continually, so especially for that particular church or Christian society whereof he himself is a member. For this he ought to wrestle with God in prayer; meantime using every means in his power to enlarge its borders, and to strengthen his brethren, that they may adorn the doctrine of God our Saviour.

Sermon 5: "On Zeal," § II.7

A Hymn from Charles Wesley

The noisy winds stand ready there
Thy orders to obey;
With sounding wings they sweep the air
To make thy chariot way.

There like a trumpet, loud and strong,
Thy thunder shakes our coast;
While the red lightnings wave along
The banners of thy host.

(*Collection—1781*, #217:5-6)

Prayers, Comments & Questions

Wisdom of God, from the street corners and at the entrances to the city you proclaim the way of life and of death. Grant us the wisdom to recognize your Messiah, that following in the way of the cross, we may know the way of life and glory. Amen.

Sunday between September 18 and 24 inclusive

Preparation for Sunday
Daily: Psalm 1

Thursday
Proverbs 30:1-10
1 Corinthians 2:1-5

Friday
Proverbs 30:18-33
Romans 11:25-32

Saturday
Ecclesiastes 1:1-18
Matthew 23:29-39

Sunday
Proverbs 31:10-31
Psalm 1
James 3:13—4:3, 7-8a
Mark 9:30-37

Reflection on Sunday
Daily: Psalm 128

Monday
Proverbs 27:1-27
James 4:8-17

Tuesday
Ecclesiastes 4:9-16
James 5:1-6

Wednesday
Ecclesiastes 5:1-20
John 8:21-38

The General Rule of Discipleship
*To witness to Jesus Christ in the world and to follow his teachings
through acts of compassion, justice, worship, and devotion under the guidance of the Holy Spirit.*

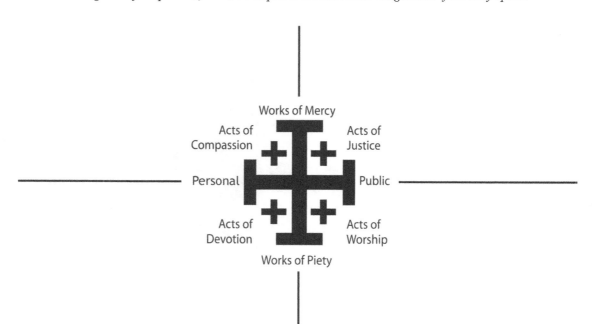

A Word from John Wesley

But [Christians] should be more zealous for the ordinances of Christ than for the church itself; for prayer in public and private; for the Lord's supper, for reading, hearing, and meditating on his word; and for the much-neglected duty of fasting. These he should earnestly recommend; first, by his example; and then by advice, by argument, persuasion, and exhortation, as often as occasion offers.

Sermon 92: "On Zeal," § II.8

A Hymn from Charles Wesley

There the rough mountains of the deep
Obey thy strong command;
Thy breath can raise the billows steep,
Or sink them to the sand.

Thy glories blaze all nature round,
And strike the wond'ring sight,
Through skies, and seas, and solid ground,
With terror and delight.

(*Collection—1781*, #217:9-10)

Prayers, Comments & Questions

God of unsearchable mystery and light, your weakness is greater than our strength, your foolishness brings all our cleverness to naught, your gentleness confounds the power we would claim. You call first to be last and last to be first, servant to be leader and ruler to be underling of all. Pour into our hearts the wisdom of your Word and Spirit, that we may know your purpose and live to your glory. Amen.

Sunday between September 25 and October 1 inclusive

Preparation for Sunday
Daily: Psalm 124

Thursday
Esther 1:1-21
Acts 4:13-31

Friday
Esther 2:1-23
Acts 12:20-25

Saturday
Esther 3:1-15
Matthew 5:13-20

Sunday
Esther 7:1-6, 9-10;
9:20-22
Psalm 124
James 5:13-20
Mark 9:38-50

Reflection on Sunday
Daily: Psalm 140

Monday
Esther 4:1-17
1 Peter 1:3-9

Tuesday
Esther 5:1-14
1 John 2:18-25

Wednesday
Esther 8:1-17
Matthew 18:6-9

The General Rule of Discipleship
To witness to Jesus Christ in the world and to follow his teachings
through acts of compassion, justice, worship, and devotion under the guidance of the Holy Spirit.

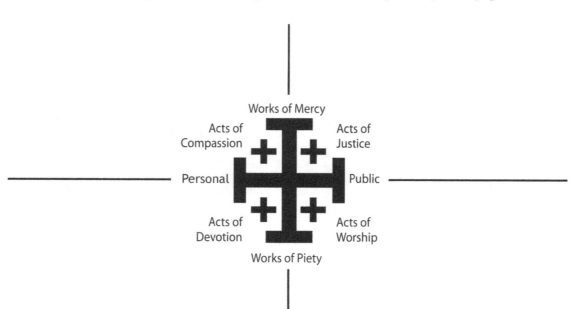

A Word from John Wesley

Thus should [Christians] show zeal for works of piety; but much more for works of mercy; seeing "God will have mercy and not sacrifice," that is, rather than sacrifice. Whenever, therefore, one interferes with the other, works of mercy are to be preferred. Even reading, hearing, prayer are to be omitted, or to be postponed, "at charity's almighty call;" when we are called to relieve the distress of our neighbour, whether in body or soul.

Sermon 92: "On Zeal," § II.9

A Hymn from Charles Wesley

Summoned my labour to renew,
And glad to act my part,
Lord, in thy name my work I do,
And with a single heart.

End of my every action thou,
In all things thee I see;
Accept my hallowed labour now;
I do it unto thee.

Whate'er the Father views as thine
He views with gracious eyes;
Jesu, this mean oblation join
To thy great sacrifice.

(*Collection—1781*, #312:1-3)

Prayers, Comments & Questions

O God, our guide and help in alien and contentious places: As Esther prayed faithfully and worked courageously for the deliverance of your people, strengthen us to confront the oppressor and free the oppressed, so that all people may know the justice and unity of your realm. Amen.

Sunday between October 2 and 8 inclusive

Preparation for Sunday
Daily: Psalm 26

Thursday
Job 2:11—3:26
Galatians 3:23-29

Friday
Job 4:1-21
Romans 8:1-11

Saturday
Job 7:1-21
Luke 16:14-18

Sunday
Job 1:1, 2:1-10
Psalm 26
Hebrews 1:1-4; 2:5-12
Mark 10:2-16

Reflection on Sunday
Daily: Psalm 55:1-15

Monday
Job 8:1-22
1 Corinthians 7:1-9

Tuesday
Job 11:1-20
1 Corinthians 7:10-16

Wednesday
Job 15:1-35
Matthew 5:27-36

The General Rule of Discipleship
To witness to Jesus Christ in the world and to follow his teachings
through acts of compassion, justice, worship, and devotion under the guidance of the Holy Spirit.

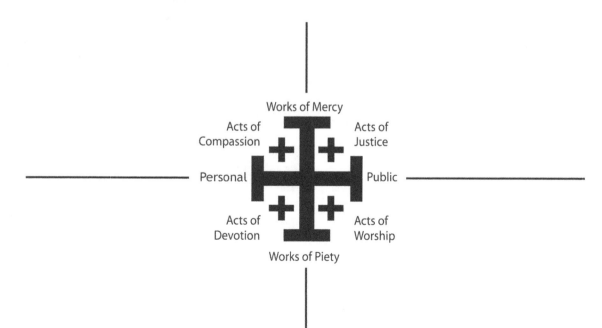

A Word from John Wesley

But as zealous as we are for all good works, we should still be more zealous for holy tempers; for planting and promoting, both in our own souls, and in all we have any intercourse with, lowliness of mind, meekness. gentleness, longsuffering, contentedness, resignation unto the will of God, deadness to the world and the things of the world, as the only means of being truly alive to God. For these proofs and fruits of living faith we cannot be too zealous. We should "talk of them as we sit in our house," and "when we walk by the way," and "when we lie down," and "when we rise up." We should make them continual matter of prayer; as being far more excellent than any outward works whatever: seeing those will fail when the body drops off; but these will accompany us into eternity.

Sermon 92: "On Zeal," § II.10

A Hymn from Charles Wesley

God of almighty love,
By whose sufficient grace
I lift my heart to things above,
And humbly seek thy face;
Through Jesus Christ the just
My faint desires receive,
And let me in thy goodness trust,
And to thy glory live.

Spirit of faith, inspire
My consecrated heart;
Fill me with pure, celestial fire,
With all thou hast and art;
My feeble mind transform,
And, perfectly renewed,
Into a saint exalt a worm—
A worm exalt to God!

(*Collection—1781*, #314:1& 3)

Prayers, Comments & Questions

Mighty and powerful God, through Jesus Christ our Savior you come to save people in all times and places, offering them new life in your presence. Give us open hearts to receive your Chosen One, that through him we may dwell with you as faithful and committed disciples. Amen.

Sunday between October 9 and 15 inclusive

Preparation for Sunday
Daily: Psalm 22:1-15

Thursday
Job 17:1-16
Hebrews 3:7-19

Friday
Job 18:1-21
Hebrews 4:1-11

Saturday
Job 20:1-29
Matthew 15:1-9

Sunday
Job 23:1-9, 16-17
Psalm 22:1-15
Hebrews 4:12-16
Mark 10:17-31

Reflection on Sunday
Daily: Psalm 39

Monday
Job 26:1-14
Revelation 7:9-17

Tuesday
Job 28:12—29:10
Revelation 8:1-5

Wednesday
Job 32:1-22
Luke 16:19-31

The General Rule of Discipleship
*To witness to Jesus Christ in the world and to follow his teachings
through acts of compassion, justice, worship, and devotion under the guidance of the Holy Spirit.*

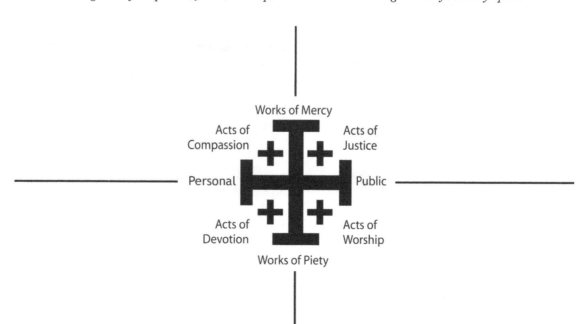

A Word from John Wesley

But our choicest zeal should be reserved for love itself, - the end of the commandment, the fulfilling of the law. The church, the ordinances, outward works of every kind, yea, all other holy tempers, are inferior to this, and rise in value only as they approach nearer and nearer to it. Here then is the great object of Christian zeal. Let every true believer in Christ apply, with all fervency of spirit, to the God and Father of our Lord Jesus Christ, that his heart may be more and more enlarged in love to God and to all mankind. This one thing let him do: let him "press on to this prize of our high calling of God in Christ Jesus."

Sermon 92: "On Zeal" § II.11

A Hymn from Charles Wesley

O thou who camest from above
The pure celestial fire t'impart,
Kindle a flame of sacred love
On the mean altar of my heart!

There let it for thy glory burn
With inextinguishable blaze,
And trembling to its source return
In humble love, and fervent praise.

Jesu, confirm my heart's desire
To work, and speak, and think for thee;
Still let me guard the holy fire,
And still stir up thy gift in me;

Ready for all thy perfect will,
My acts of faith and love repeat,
Till death thy endless mercies seal,
And make the sacrifice complete.

(*Collection—1781*, #318)

Prayers, Comments & Questions

God, you promise never to forsake us, but to bring us to life, nurture us with your presence, and sustain us even in the hour of our death. Meet us in our deepest doubts when we feel abandoned, drowning in our fear of your absence. Visit us in the tension between our yearning and our anger, that we may know your mercy and grace in our time of need. Amen.

Sunday between October 16 and 22 inclusive

Preparation for Sunday
Daily:
Psalm 104:1-9, 24, 35c

Thursday
Job 36:1-16
Romans 15:7-13

Friday
Job 37:1-24
Revelation 17:1-18

Saturday
Job 39:1-30
Luke 22:24-30

Sunday
Job 38:1-7, 34-41
Psalm 104:1-9, 24, 35c
Hebrews 5:1-10
Mark 10:35-45

Reflection on Sunday
Daily: Psalm 75

Monday
Job 40:1-24
Hebrews 6:1-12

Tuesday
Job 41:1-11
Hebrews 6:13-20

Wednesday
Job 41:12-34
John 13:1-17

The General Rule of Discipleship
*To witness to Jesus Christ in the world and to follow his teachings
through acts of compassion, justice, worship, and devotion under the guidance of the Holy Spirit.*

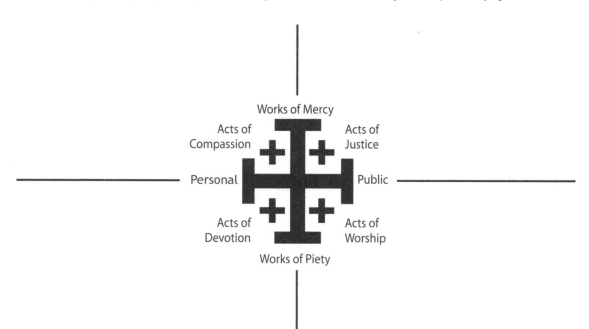

A Word from John Wesley

If zeal, true Christian zeal, be nothing but the flame of love, then hatred, in every kind and degree, then every sort of bitterness toward them that oppose us, is so far from deserving the name of zeal, that it is directly opposite to it. If zeal be only fervent love, then it stands at the utmost distance from prejudice, jealousy, evil surmising; seeing "love thinketh no evil." Then bigotry of every sort, and, above all, the spirit of persecution, are totally inconsistent with it. Let not, therefore, any of these unholy tempers screen themselves under that sacred name. As all these are the works of the devil, let them appear in their own shape, and no longer under that specious disguise deceive the unwary children of God.

Sermon 92: "On Zeal," § III.1

A Hymn from Charles Wesley

Forth in thy name, O Lord, I go,
My daily labour to pursue,
Thee, only thee, resolved to know
In all I think, or speak, or do.

The task thy wisdom has assigned
O let me cheerfully fulfill,
In all my works thy presence find,
And prove thy acceptable will.

Thee may I set at my right hand
Whose eyes my inmost substance see,
And labour on at thy command,
And offer all my works to thee.

(*Collection—1781*, #315:1-3)

Prayers, Comments & Questions

Creator God, you are wrapped in light as a garment, clothed with honor and majesty. Enlighten us with true faith and humble obedience that seeks to serve others in your name. Amen.

Sunday between October 23 and 29 inclusive

Preparation for Sunday
Daily: Psalm 34:1-8

Thursday
2 Kings 20:12-19
Hebrews 7:1-10

Friday
Nehemiah 1:1-11
Hebrews 7:11-22

Saturday
Job 42:7-9
Mark 8:22-26

Sunday
Job 42:1-6, 10-17
Psalm 34:1-8
Hebrews 7:23-28
Mark 10:46-52

Reflection on Sunday
Daily: Psalm 28

Monday
Isaiah 59:9-19
1 Peter 2:1-10

Tuesday
Ezekiel 18:1-32
Acts 9:32-35

Wednesday
Ezekiel 14:12-23
Matthew 20:29-34

The General Rule of Discipleship
*To witness to Jesus Christ in the world and to follow his teachings
through acts of compassion, justice, worship, and devotion under the guidance of the Holy Spirit.*

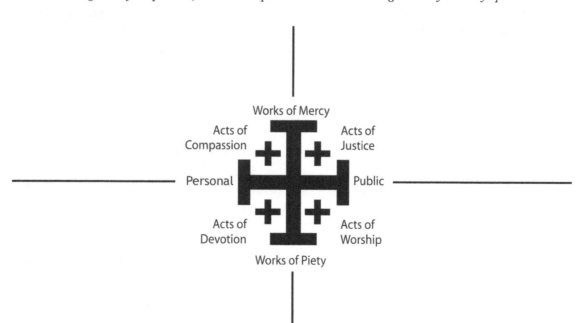

A Word from John Wesley

If lowliness be a property of zeal, then pride is inconsistent with it. It is true, some degree of pride may remain after the love of God is shed abroad in the heart; as this is one of the last evils that is rooted out, when God creates all things new; but it cannot reign, nor retain any considerable power, where fervent love is found. Yea, were we to give way to it but a little, it would damp that holy fervour, and, if we did not immediately fly back to Christ. would utterly quench the Spirit.

Sermon 92: "On Zeal," § III.2

A Hymn from Charles Wesley

Help us to help each other, Lord,
Each other's cross to bear;
Let each his friendly aid afford,
And feel his brother's care.

Help us to build each other up,
Our little stock improve;
Increase our faith, confirm our hope,
And perfect us in love.

(*Collection—1781*, #489:3-4)

Prayers, Comments & Questions

Almighty God, creator of heaven and earth in whom all things are possible, have mercy on us and heal us, that sustained by the power of your word and by the constant intercession of our Lord and Savior, we may draw near to you and follow in your way as faithful disciples. Amen.

Sunday between October 30 and November 5 inclusive

Preparation for Sunday
Daily: Psalm 146

Thursday
Ruth 1:18-22
Hebrews 9:1-12

Friday
Ruth 2:1-9
Romans 3:21-31

Saturday
Ruth 2:10-14
Luke 10:25-37

Sunday
Ruth 1:1-18
Psalm 146
Hebrews 9:11-14
Mark 12:28-34

Reflection on Sunday
Daily: Psalm 18:20-30

Monday
Ruth 2:15-23
Romans 12:17-21; 13:8-10

Tuesday
Ruth 3:1-7
Acts 7:17-29

Wednesday
Ruth 3:8-18
John 13:31-35

The General Rule of Discipleship
To witness to Jesus Christ in the world and to follow his teachings
through acts of compassion, justice, worship, and devotion under the guidance of the Holy Spirit.

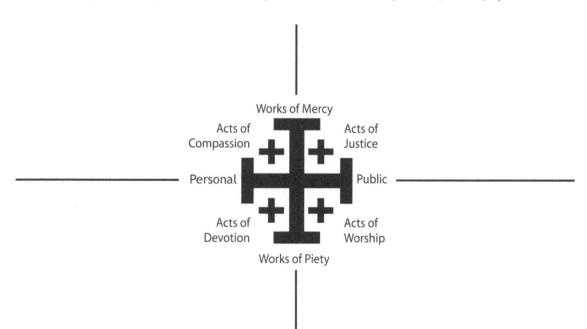

A Word from John Wesley

If meekness be an inseparable property of zeal, what shall we say of those who call their auger by that name Why, that they mistake the truth totally; that they, in the fullest sense, put darkness for light, and light for darkness. We cannot be too watchful against this delusion, because it spreads over the whole Christian world. Almost in all places, zeal and anger pass for equivalent terms; and exceeding few persons are convinced, that there is any difference between them. How commonly do we hear it said, "See how zealous the man is!" Nay, he cannot be zealous; that is impossible, for he is in a passion; and passion is as inconsistent with zeal, as light with darkness, or heaven with hell!

Sermon 92: "On Zeal," § III.3

A Hymn from Charles Wesley

Jesu, united by thy grace,
And each to each endeared,
With confidence we seek thy face,
And know our prayer is heard.

Still let us own our common Lord,
And bear thine easy yoke,
A band of love, a threefold cord
Which never can be broke.

Make us into one Spirit drink,
Baptize into thy name,
And let us always kindly think,
And sweetly speak the same.

Touched by the loadstone of thy love,
Let all our hearts agree,
And ever towards each other move,
And ever move towards thee.

(Collection—1781, #490:1-4)

Prayers, Comments & Questions

Beloved Companion, you deal with us kindly in steadfast love, lifting up those bent low with care and sustaining the weak and oppressed. Release us from our anxious fears, that we, holding fast to your commandments, may honor you with all that we are and all that we have. Amen.

Sunday between November 6 and 12 inclusive

Preparation for Sunday
Daily: Psalm 127

Thursday
Ruth 4:1-10
Romans 5:6-11

Friday
Ruth 4:11-17
Hebrews 9:15-24

Saturday
Ruth 4:18-22
Mark 11:12-14, 20-24

Sunday
Ruth 3:1-5; 4:13-17
Psalm 127
Hebrews 9:24-28
Mark 12:38-44

Reflection on Sunday
Daily: Psalm 113

Monday
Genesis 24:1-10
1 Timothy 5:1-8

Tuesday
Genesis 24:11-27
1 Timothy 5:9-16

Wednesday
Genesis 24:28-42
Luke 4:16-30

The General Rule of Discipleship
To witness to Jesus Christ in the world and to follow his teachings
through acts of compassion, justice, worship, and devotion under the guidance of the Holy Spirit.

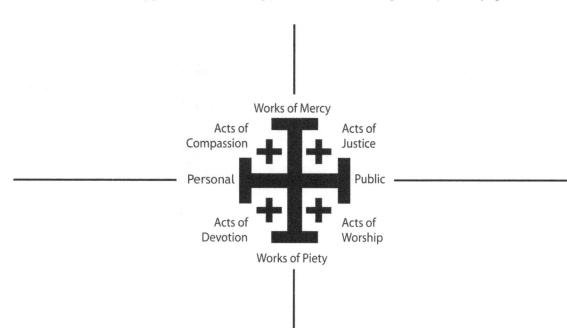

A Word from John Wesley

If patience, contentedness, and resignation are the properties of zeal, then murmuring, fretfulness, discontent, impatience are wholly inconsistent with it. And yet how ignorant are mankind of this! How often do we see men fretting at the ungodly, or telling you they are out of patience with such or such things, and terming all this their zeal! O spare no pains to undeceive them! If it be possible, show them what zeal is; and convince them that all murmuring, or fretting at sin, is a species of sin, and has no resemblance of, or connexion with, the true zeal of the Gospel.

Sermon 92: "On Zeal," § III.4

A Hymn from Charles Wesley

To thee inseparably joined,
Let all our spirits cleave;
O may we all the loving mind
That was in thee receive!

This is the bond of perfectness,
Thy spotless charity;
O let us (still we pray) possess
The mind that was in thee!

(Collection—1781, #490:5-6)

Prayers, Comments & Questions

God our redeemer, in sustaining the lives of Naomi and Ruth, you gave new life to your people. We ask that from age to age, new generations may be born to restore life and nourish the weak, by returning to you those things we once thought ours. Amen.

Sunday between November 13 and 19 inclusive

Preparation for Sunday
Daily: 1 Samuel 2:1-10

Thursday
1 Samuel 1:21-28
1 Timothy 6:11-21

Friday
1 Samuel 2:18-21
Colossians 2:6-15

Saturday
1 Samuel 3:1-18
Mark 12:1-12

Sunday
1 Samuel 1:4-20
1 Samuel 2:1-10
Hebrews 10:11-25
Mark 13:1-8

Reflection on Sunday
Daily: Psalm 3

Monday
1 Samuel 3:19—4:2
Hebrews 10:26-31

Tuesday
Deuteronomy 26:5-10
Hebrews 10:32-39

Wednesday
1 Kings 8:22-30
Mark 13:9-23

The General Rule of Discipleship
To witness to Jesus Christ in the world and to follow his teachings
through acts of compassion, justice, worship, and devotion under the guidance of the Holy Spirit.

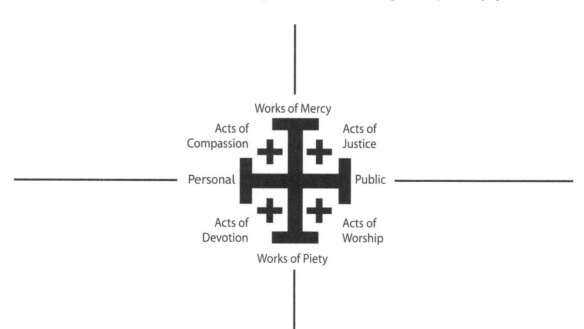

A Word from John Wesley

Take then the whole of religion together, just as God has revealed it in his word; and be uniformly zealous for every part of it, according to its degree of excellence. Grounding all your zeal on the one foundation, "Jesus Christ and him crucified;" holding fast this one principle, "The life I now live, I live by faith in the Son of God, who loved ME, and gave himself for ME;" proportion your zeal to the value of its object.

Sermon 92: "On Zeal," § III.12

A Hymn from Charles Wesley

Jesu, thou art our King,
To me thy succour bring.
Christ, the mighty one art thou,
Help for all on thee is laid;
This the word; I claim it now,
Send me now the promised aid.

High on thy Father's throne,
O look with pity down!
Help, O help! Attend my call,
Captive lead captivity;
King of glory, Lord of all,
Christ, be Lord, be King to me!

I pant to feel thy sway,
And only thee t'obey:
Thee my spirit gasps to meet,
This my one, my ceaseless prayer,
Make, O make my heart thy seat,
O set up thy kingdom there!

Triumph and reign in me,
And spread thy victory;
Hell, and death, and sin control,
Pride, and wrath, and every foe,
All subdue: through all my soul
Conqu'ring and to conquer go!

(*Collection—1781*, #342)

Prayers, Comments & Questions

God our rock, you hear the cries of your people and answer the prayers of the faithful. Grant us the boldness of Hannah, that we may persist in prayer, confident in your steadfast love. Amen.

Reign of Christ *or* Christ the King

Preparation for Sunday
Daily: Psalm 132:1-12

Thursday
2 Kings 22:1-10
Acts 7:54—8:1a

Friday
2 Kings 22:11-20
1 Corinthians 15:20-28

Saturday
2 Kings 23:1-14
John 3:31-36

Sunday
2 Samuel 23:1-7
Psalm 132:1-12
Revelation 1:4b-8
John 18:33-37

Reflection on Sunday
Daily: Psalm 63

Monday
2 Kings 23:15-25
Revelation 11:1-14

Tuesday
1 Samuel 17:55—18:5
Revelation 11:15-19

Wednesday
2 Samuel 2:1-7
John 16:25-33

The General Rule of Discipleship
*To witness to Jesus Christ in the world and to follow his teachings
through acts of compassion, justice, worship, and devotion under the guidance of the Holy Spirit.*

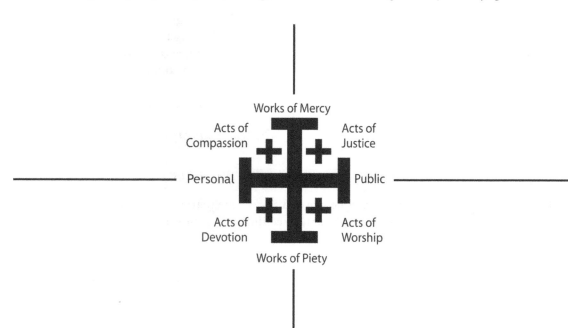

A Word from John Wesley

Be calmly zealous, therefore, first, for the Church; "the whole state of Christ's Church militant here on earth:" and in particular for that branch thereof with which you are more immediately connected. Be more zealous for all those ordinances which our blessed Lord hath appointed, to continue therein to the end of the world. Be more zealous for those works of mercy, those "sacrifices wherewith God is well pleased," those marks whereby the Shepherd of Israel will know his sheep at the last day. Be more zealous still for holy tempers, for long-suffering, gentleness, meekness, lowliness, and resignation; but be most zealous of all for love, the queen of all graces, the highest perfection in earth or heaven, the very image of the invisible God, as in men below, so in angels above. For "God is love; and he that dwelleth in love, dwelleth in God, and God in him."

Sermon 92: "On Zeal," § III.12

A Hymn from Charles Wesley

Partners of a glorious hope,
Lift your hearts and voices up.
Jointly let us rise and sing
Christ our Prophet, Priest, and King.
Monuments of Jesu's grace,
Speak we by our lives his praise,
Walk in him we have received,
Show we not in vain believed.

Hence may all our actions flow,
Love the proof that Christ we know;
Mutual love the token be,
Lord, that we belong to thee.
Love, thine image love impart!
Stamp it on our face and heart!
Only love to us be given—
Lord, we ask no other heaven.

(*Collection—1781*, #508:1, 4)

Prayers, Comments & Questions

Almighty God, you remember the oath you swore to David and so established a glorious realm of salvation through Jesus of Nazareth, his heir. Train our eyes to see your righteous rule, that, standing firmly in hope before the powers of this world, we may heed your voice and be constant in your truth. Amen.

Wesleyan Discipleship

Sermon 92: "On Zeal"

This sermon is an important word for Christians today. Wesley calls Christians to be zealous for Christ and his mission in the world. He helps us understand that true zeal is love, the love of God revealed in Christ crucified and risen. Followers of Jesus Christ are called by him to pursue holiness of heart and life, or universal love filling the heart and governing the life. SWM

"It is good to be always zealously affected in a good thing."

Galatians 4:18

Rev. John Wesley
1781

1. There are few subjects in the whole compass of religion, that are of greater importance than this. For without zeal it is impossible, either to make any considerable progress in religion ourselves, or to do any considerable service to our neighbour, whether in temporal or spiritual things. And yet nothing has done more disservice to religion, or more mischief to mankind, than a sort of zeal which has for several ages prevailed, both in Pagan, Mahometan, and Christian nations. Insomuch that it may truly be said, pride, covetousness, ambition, revenge, have in all parts of the world slain their thousands; but zeal its ten thousands. Terrible instances of this have occurred in ancient times, in the most civilized heathen nations. To this chiefly were owing the inhuman persecutions of the primitive Christians; and, in later ages, the no less inhuman persecutions of the Protestants by the Church of Rome. It was zeal that kindled fires in our nation, during the reign of bloody Queen Mary. It was zeal that soon after made so many provinces of France a field of blood. It was zeal that murdered so many thousand unresisting Protestants, in the never-to-be-forgotten massacre of Paris. It was zeal that occasioned the still more horrid massacre in Ireland; the like whereof, both with regard to the number of the murdered, and the shocking circumstances wherewith many of those murders were perpetrated, I verily believe never occurred before since the world began. As to the other parts of Europe, an eminent German writer has taken immense pains to search both the records in various places and the most authentic histories, in order to gain some competent knowledge of the blood which has been shed since the Reformation, and computes that, partly by private persecution, partly by religious wars, in the course of forty years, reckoning from the year 1520, above forty millions of persons have been destroyed!

2. But is it not possible to distinguish right zeal from wrong? Undoubtedly it is possible. But it is difficult; such is the deceitfulness of the human heart; so skillfully do the passions justify themselves. And there are exceeding few treatises on the subject; at least in the English language. To this day I have seen or heard of only one sermon; and that was wrote above a hundred years ago, by Dr. Sprat, then Bishop of Rochester; so that it is now exceeding scarce.

3. I would gladly cast in my mite, by God's assistance, toward the clearing up this important question, in order to enable well meaning men, who are desirous of pleasing God, to distinguish true Christian zeal from its various counterfeits. And this is more necessary at this time than it has been for many years. Sixty years ago there seemed to be scarce any such thing as religious zeal left in the nation. People in general were wonderfully cool and undisturbed about that trifle, religion. But since then it is easy to observe, there has been a very considerable alteration. Many thousands, almost in every part of the nation, have felt a real desire to save their souls. And I am persuaded there is at this day more religious zeal in England, than there has been for a century past.

4. But has this zeal been of the right or the wrong kind? Probably both the one and the other. Let us see if we cannot separate these, that we may avoid the latter, and cleave to the former. In order to this, I would first inquire,

I. What is the nature of true Christian zeal?
II. What are the properties of it? And,
III. Draw some practical inferences.

I.

And, First, What is the nature of zeal in general, and of true Christian zeal in particular?

1. The original word, in its primary signification, means heat; such as the heat of boiling water. When it is figuratively applied to the mind, it means any warm emotion or affection. Sometimes it is taken for envy. So we render it, Acts 5:17, where we read, "The High Priest, and all that were with him, were filled with envy,"—*eplesthesan zelou* although it might as well be rendered, were filled with zeal. Sometimes, it is taken for anger and indignation; sometimes, for vehement desire. And when any of our passions are strongly moved on a religious account, whether for anything good, or against anything which we conceive to be evil, this we term, religious zeal.

2. But it is not all that is called religious zeal which is worthy of that name. It is not properly religious or Christian zeal, if it be not joined with charity. A fine writer (Bishop Sprat) carries the matter farther still. "It has been affirmed," says that great man, "no zeal is right, which is not charitable, but is mostly so. Charity or love, is not only one ingredient, but the chief ingredient in its composition." May we not go further still? May we not say, that true zeal is not mostly charitable, but wholly so?

that is, if we take charity, in St. Paul's sense, for love; the love of God and our neighbour. For it is a certain truth, (although little understood in the world,) that Christian zeal is all love. It is nothing else. The love of God and man fills up its whole nature.

3. Yet it is not every degree of that love, to which this appellation is given. There may be some love, a small degree of it, where there is no zeal. But it is, properly, love in a higher degree. It is fervent love. True Christian zeal is no other than the flame of love. This is the nature, the inmost essence, of it.

II.

1. From hence it follows, that the properties of love are the properties of zeal also. Now, one of the chief properties of love is humility: "Love is not puffed up." Accordingly, this is a property of true zeal: Humility is inseparable from it. As is the degree of zeal, such is the degree of humility: They must rise and fall together. The same love which fills a man with zeal for God, makes him little, and poor, and vile in his own eyes.

2. Another of the properties of love is meekness: Consequently, it is one of the properties of zeal. It teaches us to be meek, as well as lowly; to be equally superior to anger or pride. Like as the wax melts at the fire, so before this sacred flame all turbulent passions melt away, and leave the soul unruffled and serene.

3. Yet another property of love, and consequently of zeal, is unwearied patience: For "love endures all things." It arms the soul with entire resignation to all the disposals of Divine Providence, and teaches us to say, in every occurrence, "It is the Lord; let him do what seems him good." It enables us, in whatever station, therewith to be content; to repine at nothing, to murmur at nothing, "but in everything to give thanks."

4. There is a Fourth property of Christian zeal, which deserves to be more particularly considered. This we learn from the very words of the Apostle, "It is good to be zealously affected always" (not to have transient touches of zeal, but a steady, rooted disposition) "in a good thing:" In that which is good; for the proper object of zeal is, good in general; that is, everything that is good, really such, in the sight of God.

5. But what is good in the sight of God? What is that religion, wherewith God is always well pleased? How do the parts of this rise one above another, and what is the comparative value of them?

This is a point exceeding little considered, and therefore little understood. Positive divinity, many have some knowledge of. But few know anything of comparative divinity. I never saw but one tract upon this head; a sketch of which it may be of use to subjoin.

In a Christian believer love sits upon the throne which is erected in the inmost soul; namely, love of God and man, which fills the whole heart, and reigns without a rival. In a circle near the throne are all holy tempers;—longsuffering, gentleness, meekness, fidelity, temperance; and if any other were comprised in "the mind which was in Christ Jesus." In an exterior circle are all the works of mercy, whether to the souls or bodies of men. By these we exercise all holy tempers; by these we continually improve them, so that all these are real means of grace, although this is not commonly adverted to. Next to these are those that are usually termed works of piety;—reading and hearing the word, public, family, private prayer, receiving the Lord's Supper, fasting or abstinence. Lastly, that his followers may the more effectually provoke one another to love, holy tempers, and good works, our blessed Lord has united them together in one body, the Church, dispersed all over the earth; a little emblem of which, of the Church universal, we have in every particular Christian congregation.

6. This is that religion which our Lord has established upon earth, ever since the descent of the Holy Ghost on the day of Pentecost. This is the entire, connected system of Christianity: And thus the several parts of it rise one above another, from that lowest point, the assembling ourselves together, to the highest, love enthroned in the heart. And hence it is easy to learn the comparative value of every branch of religion. Hence also we learn a Fifth property of true zeal: That as it is always exercised *en kalo*, in that which is good, so it is always proportioned to that good, to the degree of goodness that is in its object.

7. For example. Every Christian ought, undoubtedly, to be zealous for the Church, bearing a strong affection to it, and earnestly desiring its prosperity and increase. He ought to be thus zealous, as for the Church universal, praying for it continually, so especially for that particular Church or Christian society whereof he himself is a member. For this; he ought to wrestle with God in prayer; meantime using every means in his power to enlarge its borders, and to strengthen his brethren, that they may adorn the doctrine of God our Saviour.

8. But he should be more zealous for the ordinances of Christ than for the Church itself; for prayer in public and private; for the Lord's Supper; for reading, hearing, and meditating on his word; and for the much-neglected duty of fasting. These he should earnestly recommend; first, by his example; and then by advice, by argument, persuasion, and exhortation, as often as occasion offers.

9. Thus should he show his zeal for works of piety; but much more for works of mercy; seeing "God will have mercy and not sacrifice;" that is, rather than sacrifice. Whenever, therefore, one interferes with the other, works of mercy are to be preferred. Even reading, hearing, prayer, are to be omitted, or to be postponed, "at charity's almighty call;" when we are called to relieve the distress of our neighbour, whether in body or soul.

10. But as zealous as we are for all good works, we should still he more zealous for holy tempers; for planting and promoting, both in our own souls, and in all we have any intercourse with, lowliness of

mind, meekness, gentleness, longsuffering, contentedness, resignation unto the will of God, deadness to the world and the things of the world, as the only means of being truly alive to God. For these proofs and fruits of living faith we cannot be too zealous. We should "talk of them as we sit in our house," and "when we walk by the way," and "when we lie down," and "when we rise up." We should make them continual matter of prayer; as being far more excellent than any outward works whatever: Seeing those will fail when the body drops off; but these will accompany us into eternity.

11. But our choicest zeal should be reserved for love itself, the end of the commandment, the fulfilling of the law. The Church, the ordinances, outward works of every kind, yea, all other holy tempers, are inferior to this, and rise in value only as they approach nearer and nearer to it. Here then is the great object of Christian zeal. Let every true believer in Christ apply, with all fervency of spirit, to the God and Father of our Lord Jesus Christ, that his heart may be more and more enlarged in love to God and to all mankind. This one thing let him do: Let him "press on to this prize of our high calling of God in Christ Jesus."

III.

It remains only to draw some practical inferences from the preceding observations.

1. And, First, if zeal, true Christian zeal, be nothing but the flame of love, then hatred, in every kind and degree, then every sort of bitterness toward them that oppose us, is so far from deserving the name of zeal, that it is directly opposite to it. If zeal be only fervent love, then it stands at the utmost distance from prejudice, jealousy, evil-surmising; seeing "love thinks no evil." Then bigotry of every sort, and, above all, the spirit of persecution, are totally inconsistent with it. Let not, therefore, any of these unholy tempers screen themselves under that sacred name. As all these are the works of the devil, let them appear in their own shape, and no longer under that specious disguise deceive the unwary children of God.

2. Secondly. If lowliness be a property of zeal, then pride is inconsistent with it. It is true, some degree of pride may remain after the love of God is shed abroad in the heart; as this is one of the last evils that is rooted out, when God creates all things new; but it cannot reign, nor retain any considerable power, where fervent love is found. Yea, were we to give way to it but a little, it would damp that holy fervour, and, if we did not immediately fly back to Christ, would utterly quench the Spirit.

3. Thirdly. If meekness be an inseparable property of zeal, what shall we say of those who call their anger by that name? Why, that they mistake the truth totally; that they, in the fullest sense, put darkness for light, and light for darkness. We cannot be too watchful against this delusion, because it spreads over the whole Christian world. Almost in all places, zeal and anger pass for equivalent terms; and exceeding few persons are convinced, that there is any difference between them. How commonly do we hear it said, "See how zealous the man is!" Nay, he cannot be zealous; that is

impossible, for he is in a passion; and passion is as inconsistent with zeal, as light with darkness, or heaven with hell!

It were well that this point were thoroughly understood. Let us consider it a little farther. We frequently observe one that bears the character of a religious man vehemently angry at his neighbour. Perhaps he calls his brother *Raca*, or Thou fool. He brings a railing accusation against him. You mildly admonish him of his warmth. He answers, "It is my zeal!" No: It is your sin, and, unless you repent of it, will sink you lower than the grave. There is much such zeal as this in the bottomless pit. Thence all zeal of this kind comes; and thither it will go, and you with it, unless you are saved from it before you go hence!

4. Fourthly. If patience, contentedness, and resignation, are the properties of zeal, then murmuring, fretfulness, discontent, impatience are wholly inconsistent with it. And yet how ignorant are mankind of this! How often do we see men fretting at the ungodly, or telling you they are out of patience with such or such things, and terming all this their zeal! O spare no pains to undeceive them! If it be possible, show them what zeal is; and convince them that all murmuring, or fretting at sin, is a species of sin, and has no resemblance of, or connexion with, the true zeal of the gospel.

5. Fifthly. If the object of zeal be that which is good, then fervour for any evil thing is not Christian zeal. I instance in idolatry, worshipping of angels, saints, images, the cross. Although, therefore, a man were so earnestly attached to any kind of idolatrous worship, that he would even "give his body to be burned," rather than refrain from it, call this bigotry or superstition, if you please, but call it not zeal; that is quite another thing.

From the same premises it follows, that fervour for indifferent things is not Christian zeal. But how exceedingly common is this mistake too! Indeed one would think that men of understanding could not be capable of such weakness. But, alas! the history of all ages proves the contrary. Who were men of stronger understandings than Bishop Ridley and Bishop Hooper? And how warmly did these, and other great men of that age, dispute about the sacerdotal vestments! How eager was the contention for almost a hundred years, for and against wearing a surplice! O shame to man! I would as soon have disputed about a straw or a barley-corn! And this, indeed, shall be called zeal! And why was it not rather called wisdom or holiness?

6. It follows also, from the same premises, that fervour for opinions is not Christian zeal. But how few are sensible of this! And how innumerable are the mischiefs which even this species of false zeal has occasioned in the Christian world! How many thousand lives have been cast away by those who were zealous for the Romish opinions! How many of the excellent ones of the earth have been cut off by zealots, for the senseless opinion of transubstantiation! But does not every unprejudiced person see, that this zeal is "earthly, sensual, devilish;" and that it stands at the utmost contrariety to that zeal which is here recommended by the Apostle?

What an excess of charity is it then which our great poet expresses, in his "Poem on the Last Day," where he talks of meeting in heaven—

> Those who by mutual
>   wounds expired,
> By zeal for their distinct
>   persuasions fired!

Zeal indeed! What manner of zeal was this, which led them to cut one another's throats? Those who were fired with this spirit, and died therein, will undoubtedly have their portion, not in heaven, (only love is there,) but in the "fire that never shall be quenched."

7. Lastly. If true zeal be always proportioned to the degree of goodness which is in its object, then should it rise higher and higher according to the scale mentioned above; according to the comparative value of the several parts of religion. For instance, all that truly fear God should be zealous for the Church; both for the catholic or universal Church, and for that part of it whereof they are members. This is not the appointment of men, but of God. He saw it was "not good for men to be alone," even in this sense, but that the whole body of his children should be "knit together, and strengthened, by that which every joint supplies." At the same time they should be more zealous for the ordinances of God; for public and private prayer, for hearing and reading the word of God, and for fasting, and the Lord's Supper. But they should be more zealous for works of mercy, than even for works of piety. Yet ought they to be more zealous still for all holy tempers, lowliness, meekness, resignation: But most zealous of all, for that which is the sum and the perfection of religion, the love of God and man.

8. It remains only to make a close and honest application of these things to our own souls. We all know the general truth, that "it is good to be always zealously affected in a good thing." Let us now, every one of us, apply it to his own soul in particular.

9. Those, indeed, who are still dead in trespasses and sins have neither part nor lot in this matter; nor those that live in any open sin, such as drunkenness, Sabbath-breaking, or profane swearing. These have nothing to do with zeal; they have no business at all even to take the word in their mouth. It is utter folly and impertinence for any to talk of zeal for God, while he is doing the works of the devil. But if you have renounced the devil and all his works, and have settled it in your heart, I will "worship the Lord my God, and him only will I serve," then beware of being neither cold nor hot; then be zealous for God. You may begin at the lowest step. Be zealous for the Church; more especially for that particular branch thereof wherein your lot is cast. Study the welfare of this, and carefully observe all the rules of it, for conscience' sake. But, in the mean time, take heed that you do not neglect any of the ordinances of God; for the sake of which, in a great measure, the Church itself was constituted: So that it would be highly absurd to talk of zeal for the Church, if you were not more

zealous for them. But are you more zealous for works of mercy, than even for works of piety? Do you follow the example of your Lord, and prefer mercy even before sacrifice? Do you use all diligence in feeding the hungry, clothing the naked, visiting them that are sick and in prison? And, above all, do you use every means in your power to save souls from death? If, as you have time, "you do good unto all men," though "especially to them that are of the household of faith," your zeal for the Church is pleasing to God: But if not, if you are not "careful to maintain good works," what have you to do with the Church? If you have not "compassion on your fellow-servants," neither will your Lord have pity on you. "Bring no more vain oblations." All your service is "an abomination to the Lord."

10. Are you better instructed than to put asunder what God has joined? than to separate works of piety from works of mercy? Are you uniformly zealous of both? So far you walk acceptably to God; that is, if you continually bear in mind, that God "searches the heart and reins;" that "he is a Spirit, and they that worship him must worship him in spirit and in truth;" that, consequently, no outward works are acceptable to him, unless they spring from holy tempers, without which no man can have a place in the kingdom of Christ and God.

11. But of all holy tempers, and above all others, see that you be most zealous for love. Count all things loss in comparison of this, the love of God and all mankind. It is most sure, that if you give all your goods to feed the poor, yea, and your body to be burned, and have not humble, gentle, patient love, it profits you nothing. O let this be deep engraven upon your heart: "All is nothing without love!"

12. Take then the whole of religion together, just as God has revealed it in his word; and be uniformly zealous for every part of it, according to its degree of excellence, grounding all your zeal on the one foundation, "Jesus Christ and him crucified;" holding fast this one principle, "The life I now live, I live by faith in the Son of God, who loved ME, and gave himself for ME." Proportion your zeal to the value of its object. Be calmly zealous, therefore, First, for the Church; "the whole state of Christ's Church militant here on earth;" and in particular for that branch thereof with which you are more immediately connected. Be more zealous for all those ordinances which our blessed Lord hath appointed, to continue therein to the end of the world. Be more zealous for those works of mercy, those "sacrifices wherewith God is well pleased," those marks whereby the Shepherd of Israel will know his sheep at the last day. Be more zealous still for holy tempers, for longsuffering, gentleness, meekness, lowliness, and resignation: But be most zealous of all for love, the queen of all graces, the highest perfection in earth or heaven, the very image of the invisible God, as in men below, so in angels above. For "God is love; and he that dwells in love, dwells in God, and God in him."

The Nature, Design, and General Rules of Our United Societies

In the latter end of the year 1739 eight or ten persons came to Mr. Wesley, in London, who appeared to be deeply convinced of sin, and earnestly groaning for redemption. They desired, as did two or three more the next day, that he would spend some time with them in prayer, and advise them how to flee from the wrath to come, which they saw continually hanging over their heads. That he might have more time for this great work, he appointed a day when they might all come together, which from thenceforward they did every week, namely, on Thursday in the evening. To these, and as many more as desired to join with them (for their number increased daily), he gave those advices from time to time which he judged most needful for them, and they always concluded their meeting with prayer suited to their several necessities.

This was the rise of the **United Society**, first in Europe, and then in America. Such a society is no other than "a company of men having the *form* and seeking the *power* of godliness, united in order to pray together, to receive the word of exhortation, and to watch over one another in love, that they may help each other to work out their salvation."

That it may the more easily be discerned whether they are indeed working out their own salvation, each society is divided into smaller companies, called **classes**, according to their respective places of abode. There are about twelve persons in a class, one of whom is styled the **leader**. It is his duty:

1. To see each person in his class once a week at least, in order:
   - to inquire how their souls prosper;
   - to advise, reprove, comfort or exhort, as occasion may require;
   - to receive what they are willing to give toward the relief of the preachers, church, and poor.

2. To meet the ministers and the stewards of the society once a week, in order:
   - to inform the minister of any that are sick, or of any that walk disorderly and will not be reproved;
   - to pay the stewards what they have received of their several classes in the week preceding.

There is only one condition previously required of those who desire admission into these societies: "a desire to flee from the wrath to come, and to be saved from their sins." But wherever this is really fixed in the soul it will be shown by its fruits.

It is therefore expected of all who continue therein that they should continue to evidence their desire of salvation,

First: By doing no harm, by avoiding evil of every kind, especially that which is most generally practiced, such as:

- The taking of the name of God in vain.
- The profaning the day of the Lord, either by doing ordinary work therein or by buying or selling.
- Drunkenness: buying or selling spirituous liquors, or drinking them, unless in cases of extreme necessity.
- Slaveholding; buying or selling slaves.
- Fighting, quarreling, brawling, brother going to law with brother; returning evil for evil, or railing for railing; the using many words in buying or selling.
- The buying or selling goods that have not paid the duty.
- The giving or taking things on usury—i.e., unlawful interest.
- Uncharitable or unprofitable conversation; particularly speaking evil of magistrates or of ministers.
- Doing to others as we would not they should do unto us.
- Doing what we know is not for the glory of God, as:
  - » The putting on of gold and costly apparel.
  - » The taking such diversions as cannot be used in the name of the Lord Jesus.
  - » The singing those songs, or reading those books, which do not tend to the knowledge or love of God.
  - » Softness and needless self-indulgence.
  - » Laying up treasure upon earth.
  - » Borrowing without a probability of paying; or taking up goods without a probability of paying for them.

It is expected of all who continue in these societies that they should continue to evidence their desire of salvation,

Secondly: By doing good; by being in every kind merciful after their power; as they have opportunity, doing good of every possible sort, and, as far as possible, to all men:

To their bodies, of the ability which God giveth, by giving food to the hungry, by clothing the naked, by visiting or helping them that are sick or in prison.

To their souls, by instructing, reproving, or exhorting all we have any intercourse with; trampling under foot that enthusiastic doctrine that "we are not to do good unless our hearts be free to it."

By doing good, especially to them that are of the household of faith or groaning so to be; employing them preferably to others; buying one of another, helping each other in business, and so much the more because the world will love its own and them only.

By all possible diligence and frugality, that the gospel be not blamed.

By running with patience the race which is set before them, denying themselves, and taking up their cross daily; submitting to bear the reproach of Christ, to be as the filth and offscouring of the world; and looking that men should say all manner of evil of them falsely, for the Lord's sake.

It is expected of all who desire to continue in these societies that they should continue to evidence their desire of salvation,

Thirdly: By attending upon all the ordinances of God; such are:

- The public worship of God.
- The ministry of the Word, either read or expounded.
- The Supper of the Lord.
- Family and private prayer.
- Searching the Scriptures.
- Fasting or abstinence.

These are the General Rules of our societies; all of which we are taught of God to observe, even in his written Word, which is the only rule, and the sufficient rule, both of our faith and practice. And all these we know his Spirit writes on truly awakened hearts. If there be any among us who observe them not, who habitually break any of them, let it be known unto them who watch over that soul as they who must give an account. We will admonish him of the error of his ways. We will bear with him for a season. But then, if he repent not, he hath no more place among us. We have delivered our own souls.

The General Rule of Discipleship

The General Rule of Discipleship is a contemporary re-statement of the General Rules. It distills the General Rules down to a single, straightforward statement that can be easily memorized:

**To witness to Jesus Christ in the world and to
follow his teachings through acts of
compassion, justice, worship, and devotion
under the guidance of the Holy Spirit.**

The General Rule of Discipleship is a succinct description of discipleship. It begins by acknowledging that a disciple is one who is a witness to Jesus Christ. This tells us that he or she knows Jesus and can tell others who he is and what he is doing in the world.

A disciple lives and witnesses to Jesus Christ in the world. This acknowledges that discipleship is not primarily about the enjoyment of personal blessings. It is much more about joining Christ and his mission in the world. When Christ calls us to follow him, he calls us to follow him into the world he loves.

A disciple follows Jesus by obeying his teachings. The General Rule tells us that discipleship is a relationship with Christ. Disciples participate in practices that draw them to Christ and keep them with him. Jesus said in Luke 9:23,

> "If any want to become my followers, let them deny themselves and take
> up their cross daily and follow me."

Self-denial is loving the way Jesus loves. In the context of discipleship grace enables you to love as God loves.

The cross disciples must take up each day is obedience to Jesus' teachings summarized in Matthew 22:37-40,

> "You shall love the LORD your God with all your heart, and with all your
> soul, and with all your mind." This is the greatest and first command-
> ment. And a second is like it: "You shall love your neighbor as yourself."
> On these two commandments hang all the Law and the Prophets.

Disciples practice loving God (the cross' vertical axis) through acts of worship and devotion. They respond to God's love by loving those whom God loves, as God loves them through acts of compassion and justice (the cross' horizontal axis). As disciples take up the cross of obedience to Jesus' commands they open themselves to grace and grow in holiness of heart and life.

Finally, the General Rule of Discipleship tells us that witnessing to Jesus Christ in the world and following his teachings are guided by the Holy Spirit. This tells us that disciples cannot follow Jesus alone, by their own strength. Only the Holy Spirit, working in them by grace, makes discipleship and subsequent growth in holiness of heart and life possible.

The General Rule of Discipleship helps disciples to maintain balance between all the teachings of Jesus. This balance is represented by the Jerusalem cross (below). The support and accountability provided by a Covenant Discipleship group helps disciples to walk with Christ in the world by practicing both works of mercy (loving the neighbor) and works of piety (loving God). It also helps to maintain balance between the personal and public dimensions of discipleship.

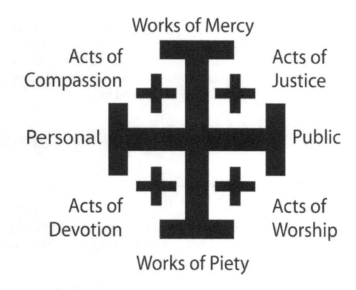

Covenant Discipleship Groups

Covenant

. . . is God's word for "relationship." Covenant is God's way of **love**. Covenant tells us that God seeks and keeps relationships with others. The nature of God's covenant is self-giving love. Jesus Christ is God's covenant love in flesh and blood. We experience this love as **grace**; responsible grace. It is God's hand, open and outstretched to the world.

Christians are people who accept God's offer of covenant love in the water of baptism. They respond by turning away from sin and accepting the freedom and power God gives to resist evil. They confess Jesus Christ as Savior, put all their trust in his grace, and promise to serve him as Lord within the community of the church. Christians understand that the life of covenant love cannot be lived alone; it requires a community of prayer, forgiveness, and love.

Christians are covenant people.

Discipleship

. . . is how Christians live out their covenant with God. It is the way of life shaped by the teachings of Jesus Christ, summarized by him in Mark 12:30-31:

> "You shall love the Lord your God with all your heart, and with all your
> soul, and with all your mind, and with all your strength. . . . You shall
> love your neighbor as yourself."

A *disciple* is a person striving to conform his or her life to the life of a beloved teacher. A disciple seeks to become *like* the teacher. Disciples of Jesus Christ are Christians who align their own desires, goals, and habits with the desires, goals, and habits of Jesus Christ.

The apostle Paul describes the goal of discipleship in Philippians 2:5,

> "Let the same mind be in you that was in Christ Jesus."

Groups

. . . are discipleship incubators. It takes a community of love and forgiveness to make disciples.

Jesus gave his disciples a new commandment:

> "Love one another. Just as I have loved you, you also should love one another. By this everyone will know that you are my disciples, if you have love for one another." (John 13:34-35)

Disciples obey this new commandment when they meet regularly in small groups. They pray for one another, the church and the world. They also give an account of how they have walked with Jesus in the world since they last met. The group works together to help one another become more dependable and mature disciples of Jesus Christ; and leaders in discipleship for the church's mission in the world.

Wesleyan Disciple-Making

Small groups that focus on mutual accountability and support for discipleship are the "method" of Methodism. These groups have their roots firmly planted in the Wesleyan tradition. The roots go even deeper when you consider that John Wesley described Methodism as his attempt to re-tradition "primitive" Christianity. He said

> "a Methodist is one who has 'the love of God shed abroad in his heart by the Holy Ghost given unto him (or her)'"—from "The Character of a Methodist"

Covenant Discipleship groups are a way of helping Christians to grow in loving God with all their heart, soul, mind, and strength and love their neighbor as themselves. They are a proven and effective way of forming **leaders in discipleship** who in turn disciple others and help the congregation to live out its mission with Christ in the world.

Covenant Discipleship groups form Christ-centered people who lead Christ-centered congregations that participate in Christ's on-going work of preparing the world for the coming reign of God, on earth as it is in heaven (Matthew 6:10; Luke 11:2).

The General Rule of Discipleship

. . . helps Covenant Discipleship group members to practice a balanced and varied discipleship. The General Rule is a contemporary re-statement of The General Rules John Wesley developed for the Methodist societies in 1742. It is simple and elegant:

> **"To witness to Jesus Christ in the world and to follow his teachings through acts of compassion, justice, worship, and devotion under the guidance of the Holy Spirit."**

Covenant Discipleship groups write a covenant that spells out how they will follow the teachings of Jesus Christ in their daily lives, shaped by the General Rule. The group's covenant serves as the agenda for the weekly one-hour meeting.

Covenant Discipleship Groups Are . . .

- up to seven persons who meet for one hour each week
- guided by a covenant they write, shaped by the General Rule of Discipleship
- where Christians give a weekly account of how they have witnessed to Jesus Christ in the world and followed his teachings, guided by the group's covenant.
- where Christians help one another become more dependable disciples of Jesus Christ.
- a proven and effective way of nurturing and identifying leaders in discipleship the church needs to live out its mission with Christ in the world.

To Learn More . . .

visit the web site at http://www.umcdiscipleship.org/covenantdiscipleship

Contact: Director of Adult Discipleship
PO Box 340003
Nashville, TN 37203-0003
Email: cdgroups@umcdiscipleship.org
Telephone: (877) 899-2780, ext. 7020 (toll free)

Recommended Resources

Accountable Discipleship: Living in God's Household by Steven W. Manskar
(ISBN: 978-0-88177-339-2)
> Provides biblical, theological, and historic foundations for Covenant Discipleship.

Disciples Making Disciples: Guide for Covenant Discipleship Groups and Class Leaders by
Steven W. Manskar (ISBN: 978-0-88177-774-1)
> A comprehensive resource for Covenant Discipleship groups and class leaders. This book will
> help them lead congregations and re-tradition classes and class leaders for today.

Everyday Disciples: Covenant Discipleship with Youth by Chris Wilterdink (ISBN: 978-0-88177-793-2)
> This book is for adult leaders of youth who are committed to helping them grow as disciples
> of Jesus Christ through discussion, action, communities of support, and mutual accountability.

Growing Everyday Disciples: Covenant Discipleship with Children by Melanie Gordon, Susan
Groseclose, and Gayle Quay (ISBN: 978-0-88177-695-9)
> This is a resource for adult guides of children. Through the model of Covenant Discipleship
> groups, children and adult guides practice their faith through holy living and modeling Jesus'
> life of caring for and serving others.

Forming Christian Disciples: The Role of Covenant Discipleship and Class Leaders in the Congregation by
David Lowes Watson (ISBN: 978-1579109462)
> This is an essential resource for pastors. Watson provides the historic, biblical, and theological
> rationale for Covenant Discipleship groups and class leaders. He helps the pastor understand
> their role in the congregation's disciple-making mission.

Help us to help each other, Lord,
Each other's cross to bear;
Let all their friendly aid afford,
And feel each other's care.

Touched by the lodestone of thy love,
Let all our hearts agree,
And ever toward each other move,
And ever move toward thee.

CHARLES WESLEY

Put your Covenant Discipleship group covenant here.

Notes

Notes

Notes

Notes

Notes

Notes

CPSIA information can be obtained
at www.ICGtesting.com
Printed in the USA
BVHW021111270323
661206BV00009B/89